JANE GIBBS
"Little Bird That Was Caught"

JANE GIBBS
"Little Bird That Was Caught"

Anne E. Neuberger
Illustrated by Tessie Bundick

RAMSEY COUNTY HISTORICAL SOCIETY
ST. PAUL, MINNESOTA

❖

Published with funds provided to the
Ramsey County Historical Society by the
Patrick and Aimee Butler Family Foundation
and the Helen Lang Charitable Trust

❖

Copy Editor: Virginia Brainard Kunz
Design & Production: Mark Odegard
Cover Illustration by Tessie Bundick:
Winona and Jane, "The Little Bird That Was Caught"
Printer: Banta
Printed in the United States of America

❖

❖

CONTENTS

Dedication

To John, Chris, Nancy, Ed, Doni, Tom,
Steve, Val, Andrea, William, and Emily

A. E. N.

And to the descendants of Jane DeBow Gibbs
and her friends among the Dakota

R.C.H.S.

A True Story

This book is based on a true story about real people who lived a long time ago. Imagine now that it is the year 1834 and that you, like Jane, are five years old. Without your parents' knowledge, you are put into a covered wagon with a family you do not know and they take you hundreds of miles away from home. Imagine that you travel on boats and live for a time in a military fort high above a mighty river. Then imagine that you arrive at a village where all the people live in houses made of tree bark or buffalo skins, and speak a language called Dakota. Imagine that you come to love the people there. You play their games, share their food, listen to their stories, and laugh and cry with them.

Then you can imagine what it was like for Jane DeBow, a white child born in New York State in 1828. She was taken from her home by another white family to a place on the far reaches of the Mississippi River that someday would be called Minnesota. There she lived near a village of the Dakota Indians on beautiful Lake Harriet in what is now south Minneapolis.

Jane DeBow not only coped with the loss of her own family, but she also adjusted to and came to love the Native American people whose lives were so unlike the lives of white families. She learned to speak two languages, to follow two sets of rules, to call two families her own, to answer to two names: her own, and *Zitkaden Usawin*, the "Little Bird That Was Caught," the name given to her by the Dakota people who knew she had been taken away from her own family and was truly a "little bird" who had been "caught" by a family not her own. She learned to live in two cultures at the same time, and while she had many painful experiences, she also had twice the adventures that most people have.

When she grew up, Jane, with her husband, Heman Gibbs, established a farm near what is now St. Paul in Ramsey County, Minnesota. Jane was truly a pioneer woman, who worked the soil and raised her children in a young country. But before that, she was a little girl who accidentally stumbled upon an adventure that would take her far from home and into the hearts of the Dakota people who lived near an army post named Fort Snelling.

So imagine now the prairie wind in your hair and the sun shining on the lake before you; come along with Jane into both of her worlds, and meet some of her real-life friends: Gideon and Samuel Pond, Chief Cloud Man, and, most of all, Winona, Great Spirit Woman, who later would be called "Nancy," meaning "grace."

Adapted by the artist from a map published in 1834. The area labeled "Huron District" is present day Wisconsin; the "Sioux District is present day Minnesota.

The Wanderer

Chapter One

The plowed soil was warm and moist but Jane's bare feet almost skimmed over it in her hurry to get home. From the Vedders' house, she could see her home each day, and that is where she wanted to be. Closer now, she could see that no doors or windows were open on this warm day, and Mama's garden, so carefully planted, was overgrown with weeds.

"Jane!" Mrs. Vedder's voice, high and strained, came over the field. "Jane DeBow, come back right now!"

Jane kept on running, her fair hair streaming behind her.

"Mama! Alzina!" she called. "Mama! Papa? Jim!"

There was no answer. The house remained silent. No big brother, no sisters called or teased. No Papa to say, "Jane, you must not wander so! Your little feet may carry you too far away!" No Mama came to stroke her hair, to sing a lullaby. There was only the wind in the wild rose bushes along the fence. Jane felt a tightness in her throat.

"Jane! Come back here right now! I cannot have you wandering off every day! You have been no end of trouble!" Mrs. Vedder was close now, her apron flapping in the breeze.

Jane knew Mrs. Vedder was angry because she was trying to make soap. Soapmaking meant tending a fire and Mrs. Vedder said each day that she could not leave it to chase Jane.

"Jane!" Mrs. Vedder had lost all patience.

"Come back with me right now!"

"Where are they?" Jane asked, not taking her eyes off the house.

Mrs. Vedder sighed. "I have told you, Jane, and I have told you! After your mama had the baby—"

"Andrew," Jane said. "His name is Andrew."

"Yes. After that, your mama was weak, and she fell—."

Of course. Jane knew. She had been there when Mama fell and could not get up. She had seen that her mother's head was badly hurt.

"And now she is in the hospital. Heavens, child, you know all of this!" Mrs. Vedder said, tugging at Jane.

"And Papa?"

"He is with your mama, a long ways away at the hospital in Rochester. Now walk by yourself, Jane! You are five years old, not a baby!"

"And Andrew? And my big sister?"

"I have told you. They are with your Aunt Rose."

"Is that where Jim and Mary are, too?" Jane asked, wondering what adventures they were having.

"Um... with your uncle. And Rosette is with your Aunt Anne. Now Jane, you know you must stay with me. You have got to stop running away. Be a good girl. I have much to do, and tomorrow we are putting up some guests."

"Oh?" Jane knew Mrs. Vedder boarded travelers from time to time. It would be fun to see new people.

"Yes! Reverend Jedediah Stevens and his family," Mrs. Vedder said. "Imagine, a minister staying with us! They are missionaries on their way west. So you be good, Jane, do you understand?"

Mrs. Vedder stopped, took a deep breath and wiped her brow with her apron.

"I want my mama," Jane said. "And my papa."

Her voice was almost carried off in the summer breeze.

"Yes, yes, I am sure you do, child, but I am doing all I can for you. Now go and play, but stay here!"

Mrs. Vedder gathered her skirts and headed to the fire she had built out-

4

side the house. Jane turned to look back at her home across the field.

The Vedders' house was warm and smelled of food cooking. Mrs. Vedder hurried around the table, placing large, steaming bowls in front of her guests. "There is plenty more. I hope you like it. Please tell me if you need anything," she said, clasping her hands tightly.

"Everything is fine," her husband said. "I think the Stevens family is ready to eat!"

"I will say grace now," said Reverend Stevens.

Everyone bowed their heads. Jane wiggled her toes and noticed how Reverend Stevens's prayer sounded like a preacher's sermon. It went on for a long time. She peeked. His eyes were closed, his mouth tight. While they appeared to be praying, the Stevens boys, Dwight and Evert, were silently, carefully, kicking each other under the table.

Jane studied the guests. Mrs. Stevens wore a traveling dress of gray, and her hair was pulled back. Jane liked the sleeves on that dress, so puffy on top, narrowing at her elbows. Mama had a dress like that, too.

Jane looked at her eyes and wondered if Mrs. Stevens was sad or just tired. Jane turned to look at

Dwight. He was about ten, the age of her brother Jim, and like Jim, he seemed full of mischief. Evert was younger, about eight, Mary's age.

Reverend Stevens seemed to loom large. He did not smile, or look at his children as her papa did at dinner. Did he even know other people were in the room?

"You have been west before, reverend?" Mr. Vedder asked.

"Oh, yes. A few years ago, I visited Fort Snelling, a military post on the upper reaches of the Mississippi River. Then I accepted a position at Fort Mackinac in Michigan territory. Two years later, I went to a place called Green Bay on the Fox River. We came back here to New York last year," he answered.

"Jedediah has been on a leave of absence. Missionary work is difficult," Mrs. Stevens added.

Jane saw the reverend's eyebrows shoot up. A looked crossed his face that made Jane think of thunder.

"We have had a rather difficult year," Mrs. Stevens added hastily.

"We have nothing but the highest regard for missionaries," Mr. Vedder said. "Spreading the word of God, so far from home, living under difficult conditions!"

Reverend Stevens smiled, and nodded. "'Therefore they that were scattered abroad went everywhere, preaching the word.' That is from the book of Acts, chapter eight, verse four."

Jane knew that was part of the Bible. Maybe if you were a preacher, you were supposed to talk about the Bible all the time.

"Jedediah was ordained this past year, so he is officially a minister now," Mrs. Stevens said. "But also, this year, our young daughter died."

"Oh, my dear," Mrs. Vedder said. "I am so sorry."

"She was about Jane's age," Mrs. Stevens said. "How old are you, Jane?" Jane held up five fingers. Mrs. Stevens looked at her with searching eyes. Jane looked down at her food.

"Where do you travel to now?" Mr. Vedder asked.

"Back to the northwest, near Fort Snelling and the Mississippi. There are groups of Sioux Indians there whom I intend to work with," Reverend Stevens responded. "We hope to arrive by the end of summer. There is no traveling once winter sets in."

"My, that must be quite far away," Mrs. Vedder said.

"Yes," Mrs. Stevens said. "It is very far away."

Jane balanced the bread on a tray as she walked slowly into the kitchen. Mrs. Vedder was washing dishes and Mr. Vedder was filling the wood box.

"She is such a refined woman, but she is so quiet. I could hardly get a word out of her!" Mrs. Vedder was saying in a loud whisper.

Reverend Stevens

"I hope she is not too refined for the wilderness she is going to have to live in," Mr. Vedder said, dropping a log into the box. "My guess is that she grew up in a well-to-do home. Not much of a preparation for the hard life her husband's work takes her to."

"Merciful heavens!" Mrs. Vedder scoffed. "She was privileged to marry such a man! Missionaries may have difficult lives, but what a lofty calling! What important work! Any girl would be lucky to make such a match."

"True," he agreed. "To be a minister's wife is an honor. I am just not sure that fancy dress will get her far in the wilderness."

He winked at Jane, who grinned back.

"Well, what about him and all that reading? He has hardly put his book down since he arrived!" Mrs. Vedder said, scrubbing a pot vigorously.

He nodded. "There will be new pleasures for them out west, I imagine. I thought I would ask him if he wanted to go for a walk, after the children are in bed."

"Good, then I can talk with her. Perhaps she will not be so quiet if we are alone. Hurry, Jane. Bring the milk out here, then upstairs with you. I want you in your nightgown right away."

Jane lay on a little bed under the eaves. She fingered the collar on the nightgown Mama had made for her. Were they back home now? She sat up and peered out the window, across the field, where she could see the house in the June twilight. There were no lights in the windows. No, they were not home yet. The night air was scented with roses, and Jane knelt by the window to feel the gentle breeze. Adult voices drifted up to her.

"It is so sad, Mrs. Stevens," Jane heard Mrs. Vedder say. "They are a kind and respectable family, but what will become of them? Surely Peter DeBow cannot care for all those children himself and keep up his carpentry work. He works nearby in Batavia at the Checkered Tavern, too. And I doubt very much that the mother will recover. Jane asks for her every day."

"Poor little one! And my baby, gone from me. Jane and I, we have our sorrows. Perhaps we could take Jane west with us!" Mrs. Stevens said. Her voice sounded happier than it had a minute earlier.

"Oh? Well, let me think about this!" Mrs. Vedder said, flustered. "Certainly, her mother can not recover, and her father would probably be relieved to have one less child to worry about. He would be glad for Jane to get such a fine family— imagine, his Jane getting a minister's family!"

"I would love to take her. She seems to be filled with wonder. Those eyes of hers! I doubt she misses much…oh, I long for my own little girl so. But I must ask Jedediah."

Jane lay back on the bed, tingling a little. Would she go west? Where was west? She had never been far from home before. Would she see those rivers the reverend talked about? Jim and Mary would surely be surprised if she was the one to have fun! Usually she had to stay home with Rosette while they left home to play. She heard the murmur of men's voices mixed with the happy tones of Mrs. Stevens. And then she slept.

The summer sun was a pale hint in the sky when Jane awoke to find Mrs. Vedder putting her clothes into a traveling bag. She sat up.

Mrs. Vedder turned to Jane. Her eyes were bright, and she sat down on the edge of the bed, something Mama would do, but never Mrs. Vedder.

She took a deep breath and said, "Oh, Jane, I have exciting news! The Reverend and Mrs. Stevens want to take you with them when they leave today! They want you to be their little girl. Their own daughter died, and they miss having a little girl. And, well, I do not think, dear, that your mama is going to get better. And your papa would probably be glad for you to have this opportunity. So I am packing your things. You do want to go, don't you, Jane?"

Go with them today? Her papa would want her to go? Jane thought for a moment. She heard voices outside the window, and looked out. There stood a covered wagon, and the reverend and his boys were arranging things in it with Mr. Vedder's help. Where would she go? What would she see?

"You do want to go, don't you, Jane?" Mrs. Vedder asked again, her eyes on Jane.

Jane looked across the field where her home stood in darkness. No, they were not home yet. She thought of Mrs. Vedder and her soapmaking. Yes, she would love to go! When she came back, she could tell her brother and sisters all about it!

Jane nodded.

"Good!" Mrs. Vedder said. "I will go tell Mrs. Stevens. She is so hoping you will come with her. Hurry now and get dressed. I have packed your clothes. You only need to eat, and you will be on your way. Imagine, Jane, you will be in a missionary family. You are a lucky girl!"

Jane pulled her clothes on so swiftly that she was on her way downstairs just as Mrs. Vedder gave Mrs. Stevens the news.

"Oh, Jane, you have made me so happy!" Mrs. Stevens exclaimed softly, her eyes shining as she hugged Jane gently. Jane smiled politely but quickly. She tried instead to see around Mrs. Stevens, to the action outside.

Breakfast was a hurried affair, after another lengthy prayer from the reverend. Jane could hardly wait to get into the wagon and go! A team of horses was harnessed to the wagon. Her small bag was lifted into it and placed among piles of trunks, barrels, and boxes. Dwight and Evert climbed into the back of the wagon, and Mr. Vedder lifted Jane in beside them.

The reverend picked up the reins, spoke to the horses, and they started off. Jane heard the good-byes from the Vedders. She turned to look back at her house, but the wagon cover was in the way so she gazed through the opening in front, ahead, to where she was going.

With each turn of the wooden wheels, Jane and the Stevens family moved slowly out of their home state of New York. All around them, trees shaded the trail, and dust settled on their trunks and boxes. As it was pleasant out, the reverend stopped to roll back the cover.

Jane, Dwight, and Evert played a game of counting animals they saw along the way.

Dwight, being the eldest, spied the most.

"A red squirrel!" he shouted.

"Where, where?" demanded Jane.

"Up there, that oak tree, up—farther up!" Dwight directed.

"I don't see it," Evert said suspiciously. "We cannot count it!"

Jane's gaze was taking in everything around her, and a slight movement in the oak showed her Dwight had indeed seen a red squirrel.

"I see it, too! I see it, too!" she shrieked with delight.

Mrs. Stevens turned from her seat in the front of the wagon and smiled at Jane.

"Better they count their blessings than

squirrels," the reverend said to his wife.

"The animals are God's creation, Father," Dwight said mildly. "We can see what God has given us here."

"When we settle again, we will go back to having the children memorize scripture each day," the reverend said to Mrs. Stevens. "'And thou shalt teach them ordinances and laws, and shalt shew them the way wherein they must walk.' Exodus, chapter 18. I will not have their studies neglected. The little girl can begin, too. She will read soon."

The wagon lumbered along, the clopping of the horses' feet and the creaks of the wagon the only noises interrupting the forest sounds. Jane listened to the wind gently stirring the trees, and the chirring of the squirrels. She noticed how green the leaves were, and that the bark on some trees was smooth, rough on others. She would have so much to tell Jim and Mary when she got back! There was a slight movement near a bush and a small, brown rabbit scurried out from under it for the shelter of a thicker bush.

"Rabbit!" Jane shouted.

"Stop the game now, children," the reverend said curtly. "We must ford a stream soon."

"How does he know?" Jane asked Dwight. It

did not occur to her to ask the reverend himself.

"See those trees?" Dwight said, pointing to trees whose long branches hung to the ground. "They are called willows, and they grow near water. So most likely there will be a stream nearby."

Soon Jane saw the glitter of early evening sunlight on water and the ground began to slope.

"It is a small stream," Mrs. Stevens said. "It should not be difficult." But Jane saw her face tighten.

The horses moved down into the stream bed and the wagon followed. They were soon through the water and the horses were straining to climb up the other bank.

"We will camp here," the reverend announced. "Dwight will help me. Evert, take the child and gather firewood."

Jane was almost jumping up and down, she was so glad to be off the wagon. It felt wonderful to stretch! She wanted to run as far and as fast as she could. She turned to follow Evert.

"Jane!" Mrs. Stevens called. "Stay close to

Evert. Do not wander so far that you cannot hear us."

Jane stopped. She remembered her father saying, "Jane, you must not wander so! Your little feet may carry you too far away!" What would Papa say when she came home?

Like a little bird, she flitted off to join Evert in their task.

The damp smell of the evening forest was lost to the delicious aroma of bacon and corncakes cooking over the fire. Jane was glad for its warmth. Evening was coming on and the shadows would soon deepen into darkness. What a

day it had been! This was much better than soap-making at the Vedders'!

The reverend bowed his head and began to pray in a quiet voice. Jane felt herself yawning. Then, something he said came through to her.

"And may the almighty Father watch over us this coming night and keep us from all harm, from wild animals, lightning, thieves, and all other dangers. We pray that we are brought safely to the morning light."

Jane's eyes widened. Darkness had crept up on her. Everything outside the firelight was mysterious and scary. Now she was too full of questions to eat. "What kind of animals? What will they do to us? Can lightning hurt us?"

"Hush, now, Jane, and eat before your food cools," Mrs. Stevens said soothingly. "Are you not hungry?"

Of course, but she was more frightened than

hungry. "Are there bears?"

"The almighty God will watch over us," the reverend said. "Eat."

Jane ate, and the food did make her feel better, but when Mrs. Stevens helped her into her nightgown, she shivered as much from fear as from the night chill. Then she heard Mrs. Stevens's kind voice saying, "Here, dear, I have made a bed for you. You are to sleep in the wagon with me. You have soft blankets to lie on, and another for a cover. I will be here, too, just on the other side of the trunk. The others will sleep near the fire. Turn, and I will button your nightgown."

"My mama made this nightgown for me. At home I sleep with Rosette." It made Jane feel safer to talk of home.

"Oh," Mrs. Stevens said flatly.

There came a ghostly call from a nearby tree, and Jane felt Mrs. Stevens stiffen.

"That is just an owl, I think," she said. "Now lie down. I hope you sleep well."

Jane did as she was told, but she went to sleep knowing that Mrs. Stevens was lying awake on the other side of the trunk.

They awoke to an overcast sky, but at least no

harm had come to them during the night. The reverend squinted at the looming clouds. "We had better travel with the cover on the wagon," he said.

"Must we, Father?" Dwight asked.

The reverend gave Dwight the same look Jane had seen at the Vedders'. A look of thunder. "You are questioning me?" he asked.

"No, Father," Dwight said quickly.

"Then help me get the cover on."

A light rain had begun to fall, but it was hot in the wagon with the cover on. Jane wished she could be outside.

"It will not be too many more days now before we are in Ohio," the reverend said. "There we will follow what is called the Main Road."

"We should have no trouble getting to Fort Snelling before winter," Mrs. Stevens said.

"Winter? We will be there by the end of summer."

"When will you take me home?" Jane asked.

The adults did not answer. Dwight leaned closer and whispered, "Tomorrow we will play the animal game again. You are better at it than Evert!" He flashed her a smile that reminded her of her brother Jim.

That night a thunderstorm crashed and boomed and Jane cried out, half asleep, half terrified.

"Hush, child. I am here," she heard a voice say.

"Mama?"

"Yes."

Jane was awake now. "No, you are not my mama. You are Mrs. Stevens. I want my mama!"

Mrs. Stevens tried to put her arms around her, but Jane pushed her away, and buried herself under her quilt. A clap of thunder shook the wagon, and there were murmurs of fear. When it was quiet, she heard Mrs. Stevens say, "She will forget."

Jane wrapped the quilt more tightly around her, to close out the thunder and the voice that was not Mama's.

The small road they followed was muddy and rutted from the rainstorm, and the horses moved slowly. Still, by nightfall they were in what the reverend called Ohio. The next morning the sun shone and the top was down. The children listened when Mrs. Stevens asked her husband, "When do you think we will reach an inn?"

"By tonight, I should think," the reverend answered.

Jane felt like a rich girl, sitting in the inn, eating supper. Soon she would curl up happily in a bed. No cramped wagon tonight! The reverend was reading at the table. Dwight and Evert ate with gusto. Mrs. Stevens looked very tired. Still she smiled at Jane when she realized the child was studying her.

"You notice everything, little Jane," she said.

"That is what my papa says," Jane said, smiling back. When she was back home, she would tell her papa what a nice lady Mrs. Stevens was. But tonight all that really mattered was that she was in this snug inn and she would sleep in a bed. Would Jim and Mary even believe that she had stayed at an inn?

When they finished eating, the reverend said, "You and the children go on up to bed. I want to stay down here for a while and read."

Mrs. Stevens nodded, motioning to the children. Jane went up the stairs, eager to see their room.

"Jane, Jane, wake up! Hurry, I must dress you," said a whispered voice.

Jane did not move. She was so tired, and it was still night, so this must be a dream. "Is it morning?" she asked sleepily.

"No, but we must leave. Be quiet now, but get up," Mrs. Stevens said, her voice fearful and stern at the same time.

Jane realized Dwight and Evert were up, too. In the dim lamplight, they looked as sleepy and confused as she felt.

"Why, Mother?" Dwight asked.

"Hush. No questions now. Just do as you are told."

Without understanding, Jane was soon in the wagon, and moving along the road in the middle of the night. In the darkness, she sensed that both the adults were frightened, and although the horses were still exhausted from the long day's travel, the reverend urged them on.

Unable to sleep, Jane lay in her quilt and cried. For hours, the reverend drove the horses on in the darkness. Finally, Jane saw a faint glimmer in the eastern sky. The pace of the horses had slowed, and no longer so afraid, Jane began dozing. In and out of a deep sleep, she heard Dwight asking questions and snatches of murmured answers.

"We had to leave because of something I heard while I was downstairs reading...a young man came in. He told the innkeeper that the night before he had met three Dutchmen from New York in an inn east of here...one of them said his little girl was in a covered wagon, just ahead...these men wanted to catch up with her...of course I came right upstairs...ordered the horses...who were they? I imagine her father, maybe her uncles, too, for the man said there were three of them..."

The sun was shining brightly when Jane fully awoke, but they paused only long enough to eat and water the horses.

Jane had dreamed of her father, and she felt sad now. She must ask again when they would take her home. She had other questions, too.

"Why did we leave the inn when it was still time to sleep?" she asked, biting into a cold corncake.

"Because it was not a safe place," Mrs. Stevens said.

"Will we stay at another inn sometime?"

"Yes, probably, but not tonight," she answered quietly. "No more questions now. Finish

eating, for we must be on our way."

"Will you take me home today?" Jane asked.

"Well, now Jane, I am so glad you are here with us. Aren't you enjoying the trip?"

"Yes, but I want to go home now."

"Jane, I need you. I need to have a little girl. I

want you to stay with me and be part of our family. Dwight and Evert will be your big brothers and I will be your mother. Now go and fetch some water and wash up while you are at the stream."

It was hotter these days, and this stream was just a trickle. Jane scooped up a cupful, then another, pouring them into the bucket. Maybe they were never going to take her home.

She stood up and looked back at the trail they had traveled. Back there, far, far back, was home. But it was such a winding road, and it was too far to walk. Besides, she could not go by herself. She remembered the prayers about wild animals, and lightning, and thieves.

She picked up her bucket and walked slowly back to the camp.

Island Winter

Chapter Two

The water stretched as far as Jane could see. It was blue and gray and she loved the aliveness of it, and the movement of the steamboat on the great lake called Michigan.

The boat had seemed huge when she and the Stevens family had boarded it in Green Bay, but now, on this endless lake, it almost felt small. She shivered a little, and pulled her coat more tightly around her. The coat was new. Mrs. Stevens had made it for her while they waited in Green Bay. She said Jane would need it on their journey north to Mackinac Island. As she watched Mrs. Stevens sew, Jane had wondered where the little coat would take her.

They had traveled so long and so far that Jane had given up asking when they would take her home. She had wandered far, far away. A few tears slipped down her cheeks and into the scarf tied under her chin. Mrs. Stevens had knit it for her, too. She was not Mama, but she was kind.

Jane remembered when the reverend had finally announced that they would soon reach Chicago. Dwight and Evert had exchanged looks. The reverend had told the children many times that they were not to ask questions, so in a low voice, Evert had asked his mother about Chicago.

"It is a large village," she answered, just as quietly. "When I went to school, Chicago was called Fort Dearborn because there was nothing there but the fort, and a few other buildings. Now it is a real town with about two hundred wooden buildings. It is on Lake Michigan."

"Father thinks we can get to Fort Snelling before winter. Do you think so, Mother?" Dwight asked.

"Your father has traveled there before, so he

must know best," she said. Jane watched her pick nervously at the fringe on her shawl. "But if we cannot, he will make other plans. We could go back to Mackinac Island."

They had traveled through Chicago, and on to a place called Green Bay, where the reverend once had preached. Dwight told Jane and Evert that to get to Fort Snelling they would travel by boat through rivers, but then, in the month of August, the rivers had been too low to float a boat. So they had waited in Green Bay. From the heat of August to this cool day in October, they had waited for the waters to rise.

Finally Reverend Stevens had announced that they could not wait any longer. They would spend the winter on the island called Mackinac, which lay between two huge lakes, Michigan and Huron, and they would reach it by steamer. He would work with the mission there, and the family would have a house to live in. They would be warm and safe this winter.

Mrs. Stevens had given a sigh so loud everyone looked at her. Casting her eyes down, she said quietly, "I am so glad you have decided this, Jedediah."

So they had boarded the boat, and now Jane felt the misty air against her forehead and cheeks as the waters rolled in front of the boat.

"Aren't you cold?"

Jane turned to see Dwight standing there.

She nodded but smiled. "I like it here."

"Mother says you should come down if you are cold," he said dutifully, but he, too, began watching the endless waves.

"The water always changes, every minute," Jane observed, her eyes wide. "It is even better than the clouds! Is it a long way to Mackinac Island?"

"Yes. We lived there before, you know, when Evert and I were small."

"Tell me about it! Please?" Jane asked.

"I do not remember too much," Dwight said, shivering a little, "There is a fort there, but we will live in a building called the Mission House. It is a boarding school and some children live in part of it, and go to school there, too. We will live in a different part of the house, and I heard Father say we will go to school in the bottom floor of the church. It is not too far to walk—even as little boys we walked to church from there."

"Why don't we go to school at the Mission House?" Jane asked. She liked thinking about going to school.

"The school there is for children whose

fathers work at the big fur trading company. I do not think they speak English, though their teachers teach it to them."

Jane's eyes widened again. "What do they speak?"

Dwight grinned. "It is funny, but the girls speak Ojibwa, like their mothers, and the boys speak French, like their fathers. That I remember. But they did talk to each other somehow, and I do not remember them ever speaking much English."

Silent now, Jane wondered what it would be like to learn another language. Then she asked, "Can we play with them?"

"I was too little to when I was there last, but probably not. Father probably will not want us to," Dwight said, then stood up. "Father and Evert are ill with the movement of the ship. I am going down. Come down if you get colder. Mother does not want you getting chilled."

"I am fine."

"Mother is right about you. You notice everything. That is why you are up here, for there is nothing below to see. But at least it is warm!" Dwight said, and with a grin he left.

Jane remained alone, gazing out upon the vast waters, waiting for what life would bring her next.

She saw the autumn colors first. The island was still some distance off, but she could see it was covered with trees in a riot of fall color.

"See all the pretty leaves!" Jane exclaimed.

Mrs. Stevens smiled down on her. "God's creation is certainly beautiful," she said.

"Let God guide us safely through the straits. Let us pray that we reach the island without any problems," the reverend said. "It is narrow and dangerous."

The family prayed, but Jane did not worry about the reverend's fearful warnings. Too many nights she had gone to bed frightened, and awakened to find everything was fine.

As they neared the island, Jane saw a long wall jutting out from the top of the hill. There were buildings behind it, and a flag flew from it. Was that the fort Dwight had mentioned? How far was it to the Mission House?

Jane marveled at the number of people near the boat landing. They were all dressed differently from each other and from the people on the boat. Evert poked her.

"Look!" he whispered. "Those men are soldiers, and the ones over there are sailors."

"Who are those people?" Jane asked, pointing.

"Sh! And do not point!" Evert scolded. "Some are fur traders. They speak French."

"Oh, look!" Jane exclaimed. She saw two men with leather leggings and fur blankets around

their shoulders. Both wore their hair in a braid, and one man had feathers tucked into his. She could not take her eyes off them. "Who are they?"

"They are Indian men!" Evert answered. "Those are the people my father helps. The Indian people here are called 'Ojibwa'."

"Hush, children," Mrs. Stevens said, approaching them. "And do not gawk at people. We are ready to leave the boat."

Jane took one last look at the men standing in the October wind. They seemed strong and healthy. Why would the reverend have to help them? It did not seem that they needed any help.

The boat reached the landing. Jane and Evert jumped, giggling as their feet hit earth once more. As baggage was unloaded from the boat, they began a chasing game.

"Be still, children, and silent!" the reverend said stormily. "'The way of the slothful man is as a hedge of thorns, but the way of the righteous man is made plain.' Find that in Proverbs, Evert, when the Bible is unpacked. But for now, make yourselves useful by gathering our bags." The reverend walked off to make inquiries.

Jane looked up the hill to the long wall on top of it. It was so very high! Now she could see the

34

nose of a cannon poking out from the wall, and the flag flapping merrily in the wind.

"Is that the fort?" she asked. "Is that why there are the soldiers here?"

Stacking bags, Evert nodded, saying, "You had better help, Jane."

Jane shrugged. There was always work, but now was a time to wonder.

They were taken by wagon along the main street near the landings. Jane was delighted to see several buildings and houses along this street.

"There is the home of the Stuarts!" Mrs. Stevens said.

Jane looked at her. Usually, she thought, Mrs. Stevens sounded tired or worried, or she was just quiet. Now she seemed happy.

"Do you think Elizabeth and Robert are still here?" she asked eagerly.

The reverend shrugged his shoulders. "Perhaps. He is still the manager of the American Fur Company here and Mackinac is the headquarters for the whole region. I do know the Reverend and Mrs. Ferry are gone. And good riddance, I say."

"Jedediah!" Mrs. Stevens exclaimed. "I know you and Reverend Ferry did not agree on certain matters, but he and Amanda did begin the school here and..."

"I am only glad I do not have to work with him this winter. Enough said on the matter. I am glad to see that the church still stands," he answered, pointing ahead.

Jane peered farther up the road to see a pretty white building with many steps leading up to it. Windows with tiny panes flanked both sides of the door.

"Look at the steeple!" Jane exclaimed. High above the door, pointing to the sky, was a square tower topped by a smaller, six-sided tower with a weather vane at the very peak.

"It is good," the reverend said.

Startled, Jane paused to look at him. The reverend rarely answered her. He was gazing at the impressive steeple.

"'Yea, woe is unto me, if I preach not the gospel,' First Corinthians. I look forward to preaching here," he said to his wife.

"I am glad, Jedediah," she said. "It will be a good winter, I think."

The wagon rolled on.

They settled into the Mission House, a short

walk uphill from the church. Jane loved the building, which was huge, bigger than the Checkered Tavern where her father worked back in New York.

It had three sections. Had Jane known her letters better, she would have seen that it was like a large letter "I". The west wing was where the Stevens family and Jane settled. They lived mainly in a large room with a fireplace. The reverend chose a room he called his study, and he disappeared into it frequently. Jane delighted in her bedroom, a tiny place cozy from the warmth of the chimney. And often she would prop her elbows on the window sill, gazing out to the water stretching as far as she could see.

Dwight was right: Reverend Stevens did not allow Jane and his sons to play with the other children who lived and learned in the rest of the Mission House. Sometimes she could hear their chatter as they climbed the stairs, and often she watched them out the window. They seemed like all other children, playing and laughing. Jane admired their dark hair and listened to their conversations, trying to understand the words floating to her.

She did have her own school now.

Her throat hurt the first day as she remembered that if she were home, she would have walked to school with her brother Jim and sister Mary.

She kept trying to swallow as Mrs. Stevens tied her scarf under Jane's chin and shooed her out the door with Dwight and Evert into the November grayness.

Scuffling through the fallen leaves, Jane forgot her sadness. She was eager to get to school.

"Girls sit on one side, boys on the other," Dwight told her. "The teacher will show you where he wants you to sit. If you stay quiet and do not wiggle too much, you will be fine."

And Jane was fine. She sat on a bench close to the fireplace with the other little girls, and listened as a young man taught each group. There was reading, history, arithmetic, geography, and handwriting. She worked on her letters, hoping that someday soon she could put them together into words. She worked on numbers, too.

Every day they prayed together, and at noon Dwight crossed over to the girls' side and handed Jane a small package. Each time she unwrapped it, she found two corncakes spread with maple sugar. Jane ate them hungrily, then rushed out to play with the other children in the wintery air.

There was a routine at home now, too. Every

morning before breakfast, Dwight and Evert opened
the family Bible, for they were required by their
father to learn a line from scripture each day before
they could eat. The reverend first looked to Dwight.

"'The kingdom of heaven is like to a grain of
mustard seed, which a man took, and sowed in his
field'," Dwight said quickly.

His father nodded, then turned to Evert.
"'Teach me thy way, O Lord; I will walk in thy
truth'," Evert recited.

"Good," the reverend said, and then they
could begin to eat. Jane knew that as soon as she
could read, she, too, must memorize lines. She was
looking forward to reading the Bible stories Mrs.
Stevens told her, stories about Noah, Joseph, and of
course, Jesus.

Usually, Reverend Stevens was silent as he ate,
but once he said as if to himself, "It is good to hear
the children learning the holy words. May the good
Lord help me reach the heathens, so that they, too,
may become children of God."

No one responded. Jane wondered who these
heathens were, but now was not the time to ask.

"It has been decided, Julia," Reverend Stevens
said to his wife. "I am to lead a revival, as I had

hoped. We will begin next week."

"Oh, Jedediah! That is wonderful," Mrs. Stevens said, her eyes shining. "Truly, the Lord wanted us to be here this winter!"

"What is a revival?" Jane whispered to Evert who was shooting marbles across the floor.

"It is many church services in a few days where my father preaches. If it is a good one, many people come and they join the church then," Evert whispered back. "And it means that we go to church many times next week."

Sunday dawned bleak and cold. Snowflakes flurried in the air as Mrs. Stevens and the children walked down the hill towards the church. Reverend Stevens was already there. Jane noticed that the lake was steel gray. She marveled at the beauty of a snowflake that landed on her dark coat.

Inside the church, Evert whispered, "It is almost as cold in here as it is outside!"

"At least I will not fall asleep this time!" Dwight said, good naturedly.

The two boys grinned at each other. Once in the warmer months, Dwight had become so drowsy in the heat of a long church service that he had fallen asleep. That afternoon, he had been thrashed by his father.

"Hush!" Mrs. Stevens said, leading the way into the church.

They were the first to arrive. All was silent. Pews lined the walls, low, orderly, and starkly plain. Everything seemed very low here to Jane, who liked to look at the sky, the trees, or the lake.

Each pew had its own little door. Dwight opened one and the family filed in. Behind them, Jane could hear other people entering the church, the small doors on the pews opening and shutting. She peeked around, knowing Mrs. Stevens was hoping many people would come. Soldiers arrived, as did others from the fur company.

Then some women entered who had long black hair that was neatly braided and shone as if it had been oiled. They wore simple dresses of deerskin decorated with pretty dyes from berries. Heavy fur-lined blankets of hide covered their shoulders and their embroidered moccasins were also fur-lined. Jewelry made of shells adorned their necks. They were Ojibwa women, Jane realized, some of the people the reverend was going to help. Well, here they were at the revival. How would he help them?

Noticing Jane turned in her seat, Mrs. Stevens sharply slapped her on the knee. Jane hastily faced the front. She did not turn around again the whole service. Instead, she concentrated on the rise and fall of Reverend Stevens' voice as he preached, and watched his eyebrows go up and down.

Jane did not know if she liked the revival or not. It meant sitting for long periods in the cold church, not daring to wiggle. The reverend had warned the children that he would be watching them from the pulpit and he expected only the best behavior. Still, Jane was not sure he really watched them, for he worked hard as he preached. Sometimes his voice was very loud and he shouted, "'For if ye live after the flesh, ye shall die'."

Then his voice dropped low, and people strained forward to hear him as he whispered, "'For the wages of sin is death'!"

He spoke as though he were talking to Jane herself, "You, yes you, must repent of your sins!" Now the reverend was leaning so far forward on his pulpit that Jane wondered if he might fall. "Any departure from the good, however small, however slight, is an offence against God. And any offense, however small, is the beginning of the worst. This small offense should be seen as an enormous crime!" he thundered, standing up, then throwing himself backward, his arms in the air to show just how big a sin could become.

Jane swallowed and vowed she would be good, right here, right now.

Then the others in the church began clapping, and agreeing loudly! Jane looked wide-eyed at them. Were they allowed to talk in church? Wasn't this a sin? Cautiously she looked at Mrs. Stevens. She was quiet, but smiling. All this pleased her.

"Come!" the reverend was booming. "Come, all you who are anxious to be saved!" He gestured to a pew close to the front. The clapping continued, and a few people hurried up. Others walked up slowly and cautiously.

Again Jane looked at Mrs. Stevens. Were they to move, too? But the Stevens family stayed where they were. Perhaps, Jane thought, they were saved already.

What had they been saved from? The clapping continued, a song followed. Jane sat rigidly in her seat. Whatever she was saved from, she was not going to commit a terrible crime by beginning to wiggle.

One day in school Jane watched as the older children practiced handwriting. In very large and curving letters that seemed to flow like a stream of water, were the words, "Cherish kind feelings."

Over and over they wrote the words, trying to perfect the letters. "Cherish kind feelings. Cherish kind feelings."

She could read!

The cold weather had set in, and with it came snow although the lake still lay open, cold and forbidding. Others told Jane that the waters near them would freeze shut by January.

But the evenings were warm in the Mission House, and Jane loved the after-supper hours when the reverend retired to his study and Dwight or Evert threw fresh logs on the fire. They sat near the fire, studying by its friendly light. Mrs. Stevens would light a candle, and repair Dwight's ripped pants or mend a hole in Evert's coat by its light. Sometimes she knit, often making socks. Jane sat near her, folding strips of paper into what Mrs. Stevens called "lighters," for they had no matches.

The fire crackled and sent playful shadows on the wall.

Christmas came quietly as usual. Mrs. Stevens was touched by the gifts of food brought in by other women living on the island. Jane and the boys were delighted, too.

At church, the reverend talked of the miracle of Jesus' birth, a story Jane loved. She sat straight in her pew, listening, but soon she was thinking of Christmas in another place and remembering a different baby, a little brother named Andrew.

Ice lay across the narrow waters that they had crossed in October. Where there was open water near the shore, wind and water would pound the steep hills on the edge of the island. The stillness of the ice and the insistence of the bitter wind made life seem small, closed, as if it had come to a halt.

In the silence of the late afternoons, she practiced her writing, trying to copy the rounded, flowing letters her teacher had shown her.

"Keep good company. Keep good company. Keep good company," she wrote over and over.

Evert lay on the floor, spinning his wooden top. Dwight came in.

"Let's go upstairs and look for the Runner!" he suggested.

The two boy scrambled up the stairs. Jane, not knowing who or what the Runner was, dashed up after them.

She found them looking out over the frozen water.

"Is that a person?"

"Where?"

"Out there, far out, to the left...."

"No, it is not moving."

"What are you looking for?" Jane demanded, peering out the small-paned window. The ice lay blue and gray over the lake.

"The Runner," Evert said, disappointment in his voice. "It will be dark soon, so he will not come today."

"But it stays light longer now," Dwight said

hopefully. "He will come soon."

"Who?" Jane insisted. "Who is the Runner?"

"A man who left the island with letters people here wrote. Mother and Father sent mail with him, too. He is going all the way to Detroit, and he will come back with mail for the islanders," Dwight said, still peering out into the gathering dusk. "He left here with a pack on his back, his snowshoes, and skates. He could come through the woods, but we expect he will come over the ice."

Jane imagined skating over the vast ice alone, with only the wind for company. This Runner must be very brave.

They heard heavy footsteps on the stairs and Reverend Stevens came into the room. He saw the children gathered around the window.

"Are you looking for the Runner?" he asked.

"Yes, Father," Evert said.

"No sign of him yet?"

Dwight shook his head.

The reverend, too, looked out the window and was silent.

Each day they looked for the Runner, but the ice remained empty.

One evening, Jane and Mrs. Stevens were

clearing the table from supper when the door burst open. Startled, Jane looked up to see Louie, the man who brought them firewood. He was almost breathless as he announced, "The Runner has come!" Then he left quickly to tell others the news.

"Wife!" Reverend Stevens called. "Bring me the lantern! Dwight, my great coat! I am going to the fort."

When the door closed behind him, Evert breathed a peephole into the frost that etched the windows. Jane and Dwight joined him to watch the lantern, all they could see of the reverend, bobbing down the hill, as he threaded his way in the darkness to the road.

It was, in a way, the end of winter, and the end of their island time.

The mail brought news of visitors coming! Jane knew none of them, though she heard names like Cousin Lucy, Miss Sarah, and Dr. Williamson.

She went to school through the snow, but the sun felt warmer on her cheeks. Icicles dripped from the Mission House roof in the afternoon.

One morning, as she sat on her bench at school, she heard a low groaning sound. Frightened, she looked up. Everyone else was looking around, too. The teacher went to the window, peered out and announced, "The ice is beginning to break up on the lake!"

The students all gave a cheer, and their teacher did not even tell them to be quiet and study!

Over the next few days, a warm wind blew and great chunks of pitted gray ice piled up near the shores. Then one day the lake was clear and Mrs. Stevens told Jane she must stay home from school to help her prepare for company.

Together they swept the cold upstairs bedrooms. Mrs. Stevens was cutting heavy paper to put up over the windows, for they had no curtains, when there was a knock at the door.

"That will be some soldiers from the fort with extra blankets. Hurry down, Jane, to let them in," she said. "And do not forget to curtsey!"

Jane opened the door. Two uniformed soldiers addressed her politely, and she made an awkward curtsey. Behind them was a pony carrying a pack of blankets, which they unloaded and carried into the house. Mrs. Stevens came down the stairs, and one solider addressed her, "A present from the sutler, Madam."

He handed her a flat tin box. Then, with a respectful touch of their caps, the soldiers were gone.

"Dried apples! This is a surprise!" she exclaimed, opening the tin. "I will make pies, as soon as we have finished making the beds."

Later, Jane stood on a chair to watch her deftly rolling out pie crusts. Gently she folded a crust and eased it into a pie pan, crimping the edges.

Jane suddenly remembered seeing this before, a long, long time ago.

Mrs. Stevens spooned some applesauce into the waiting crust, and turned happily to Jane. "You have been so much help, dear, that I will make you a saucer pie."

The memory grew stronger. Jane could hear the voice and even the words of that other pie-maker, "There is to be a saucer pie for my little girls!" Mama. Mama would make pies, and sometimes she would make a tiny one for Jane to share with Rosette.

"Goodness, Jane, you look so sad! And I am making you a treat!" Mrs. Stevens exclaimed.

"Thank you," Jane answered.

A sharp whistle pierced the air.

"Steamboat!" they heard a shout from outside.

After the quiet winter, the excitement of

having visitors seemed to fill every corner of the big house. Jane watched shyly as Cousin Lucy, the reverend's niece, and Dr. and Mrs. Williamson, and Mrs. Williamson's young sister, Sarah Poage, arrived, bringing news for the Stevens family.

People who worked on the island came to meet the visitors. The captain from the fort and several lieutenants called. Jane's teacher came, too. There was much talk and laughter. Best of all for Jane and the boys, there were wonderful meals. Sitting at the "second table," where they must wait for the leftovers from the main table, they feasted on roast venison, hominy, potatoes, and apple pie.

April was waning. Everywhere signs of new life touched the island. It was not yet warm, and mud and bits of old snow still hampered the walk to school and church, but spring was arriving. Jane was told to play outside now, as Mrs. Stevens was busy with the guests.

Still, Jane was aware that the reverend was talking seriously now with the company about something she sensed was important. Mrs. Stevens seemed excited, uncertain.

One morning, Jane was opening the Bible. Now she, too, must learn a line before breakfast.

Evert whispered, "Here, learn this!"

She felt a scrap of paper being pressed into her hand. Uncrumpling it, Jane saw it was a Bible verse. As she set the table, she memorized it.

When the family was seated, grace was said.

"Dwight?" his father said.

"'Speak unto the children of Israel that they go forward'."

"Evert?"

"'Get thee out of thy country unto a land that I will show thee'."

The reverend looked startled and Mrs. Stevens, too, seemed amazed. "Jane?" he asked.

"'He said, let us go and I will go before thee'," Jane recited easily.

A smile spread across the reverend's face. "The children have settled the question! The Lord has spoken through them. We will leave here on the next boat," he announced.

Jane, uncertain how the Lord had spoken through her, looked to Evert and Dwight. They were hunched over their plates, trying very hard not to laugh.

It was April 24, 1835.

Dressed in a new linsey-woolen dress made by Cousin Lucy, Jane and the others boarded the steamboat bound for Green Bay. Excitedly, Dwight and Evert roamed around the deck, waiting for the paddle to begin moving, peeking into the engine room. Jane was content to sit by the women, Cousin Lucy, Miss Sarah, Mrs. Williamson, and Mrs. Stevens, and listen to their conversation.

The engine started up and Jane felt the movement beneath her. She turned to watch the island grow smaller as the boat slipped farther and farther into the deeper waters of Lake Michigan.

River Travels

Chapter Three

A t Green Bay, the Fox River looked small to Jane after Lake Michigan. Still, she was happy to be boarding the boat that would take them up the river. Now they could go all the way to Fort Snelling by boats and rivers. And, best of all, they were traveling with many people. No cramped wagon for this trip!

Jane, dressed again in her new linsey-woolen dress, listened as the reverend counted off the party for the man in charge of the boat and the boatmen the reverend had hired.

"In my group, there will be nine: myself and wife, my niece, our two young sons, Dr. and Mrs. Williamson, her sister, and a little girl," he stated.

"How old are the children?" the man asked.

"My sons are eleven and nine."

"And the girl?"

"Oh, eight or nine."

Jane looked around happily. Where was this girl? She wanted to meet her! But there was no other girl. The reverend, she realized, had meant her. He did not even know how old she was.

"I am six years old," she said shyly, but no one heard her.

Now the bustle of loading the boat began. They stowed their traveling bags under the rough benches and sat down.

The boat pulled away from the shore, leaving Green Bay behind.

"The Fox River has a swift current, and it flows north," a boatman said to the reverend. "We will encounter many rapids and will have to portage around them. Tonight we should reach the Kakalin, the first of several rapids between here and Lake Winnebago. In about thirteen miles we will reach the Grand Chute, a great rapid. Its foaming waters are something to see, but it is dangerous, too."

Jane and Evert listened. "What does portage mean?" Evert asked Jane.

Jane shrugged. There was a lot to wonder about, but she had learned to watch when she had a question.

For now, she watched from her seat the grasslands dotted with majestic oak trees pass by.

Jane delighted in the company of the women, as did Mrs. Stevens, who chatted happily. They were all kind to Jane, but she especially liked Cousin Lucy.

The reverend had said Lucy was talkative, but not silly. He approved of his niece, but Jane was not sure how he felt about Miss Sarah, who cried easily and seemed uncertain about this new life she was approaching. Not Lucy, who talked strongly of her missionary work, and the importance of spreading God's word.

As the boat moved southward, Lucy began describing a book that had been published a year earlier. "It is the first book ever published in this area! I saw it myself in Green Bay. It is an almanac and was written by Father Samuel Mazzuchelli. He is a priest, a scientist, and an architect."

Miss Sarah exclaimed, "He must be well-educated!"

"Yes," Mrs. Stevens mused. "Jedediah is well-educated, too. Most of the Presbyterian ministers are, you know."

Lucy nodded. "Yes, and the Baptists, too."

"Dr. Williamson is not ordained, but he is a medical doctor, which makes him well-suited for missionary work, also," Mrs. Williamson said quickly.

Jane listened, noting how tight Mrs. Stevens's lips looked just now.

Then, more brightly, Mrs. Stevens said, "I am sure there will be plenty of work for both of them when we finally arrive!"

Miss Sarah sighed.

"Just think of the good we will do!" Lucy said enthusiastically. "Back East, they are concentrating on distributing Bibles. And in the East, in Presbyterian churches, women are praying aloud in weekday meetings when they feel the urge to do so!"

Mrs. Williamson agreed.

"Giving away Bibles!" Miss Sarah said. "To whom? Do you think the heathens will be able to read them? And women praying aloud? Who do you think will be there besides us?"

Mrs. Williamson yanked impatiently at her ball of yarn. "Oh, hush, Sarah, with your gloom. Look on this as an adventure, and stop this constant complaining!"

There was an uncomfortable silence, as Miss Sarah turned to look out of the boat. Jane saw a few tears slipping down her cheeks.

The land had changed. There were forests, hundreds of trees budding out with pale green leaves. The May weather was pleasant, and Jane breathed in the fragrance of blossoms near the shore. The Fox River widened and they passed through a beautiful lake.

"This is lovely," Mrs. Stevens said to the reverend.

"This is Butte des Morts lake, which means 'Hillock of the Dead'," he said. "The boatman told me a battle was fought here many years ago between the French and the Fox Indians. That is wild rice growing along the shore over there. In the fall, the Indian women will harvest it."

At noon they ate a dinner of roast venison and little pancakes the French boatmen called crepes. They were a long way from Mackinac Island now. Jane remembered a dark winter's night when the reverend had come out of his study with a map. Spreading it carefully on the table, he had said, "I will show you the journey we are going to take."

Standing on tiptoe, Jane had watched and listened. With his finger, the reverend traced a line from Green Bay and the Fox River to a portage, a place where they would cross over to the Wisconsin River. They would take the boat down the Wisconsin to a settlement called Prairie du Chien. Jane had loved the sound of that name. She wondered what a place called Prairie du Chien might look like.

Still, their journey would not be over. The reverend had said they would wait for yet another boat, a steamboat that would be heading north on a river called the Mississippi, and to a military post called Fort Snelling.

"While we are there, I will decide where to build a Mission Station," he had said solemnly. He folded up the map then and returned to his study.

That winter night seemed far away.

Now she heard voices. It was Mrs. Williamson and her sister. They did not see her, but sat down with their knitting.

Miss Sarah said, "There is something odd about the Stevens child. Have you noticed? She never calls Mrs. Stevens 'mother,' as the boys do. And one day, Jane told me she has a baby brother named Andrew!"

"A younger brother? Andrew?" Mrs. Williamson asked, puzzled.

"And when I was wearing my turquoise beads, little Jane said to me, 'My mama wears beads like that.' So I said, 'You mean Mrs. Stevens?' and she said, very firmly, 'No, my mother'."

"Now that you mention it, I overheard Mrs. Stevens tell Lucy that her name is Jane DeBow Stevens," Mrs. Williamson said.

Jane was about to jump up to shout that her name was Jane DeBow, when she heard Cousin Lucy approaching.

"Lucy," Miss Sarah said, "is little Jane your cousin?"

"Well, she was not born to Aunt Julia and Uncle Jed. They did have a little girl, who died a few years ago. I think they adopted Jane, but perhaps not. I am not certain, as no one in the family seems willing to talk about it."

"Well," Miss Sarah said. "There is something sad about her."

"Oh, posh, Sarah!" Mrs. Williamson said stoutly. "She is a perfectly happy little girl!"

"She reminds me of a little bird, always watchful, always noticing," Miss Sarah added.

"That," said Lucy, "is a sign of intelligence!"

"Evert," said Cousin Lucy, after they had eaten breakfast. "What river are we on?" She said it as if she were their teacher.

"The Fox River," Evert answered.

"And how do you spell that?"

"F-O-X," Evert said.

"Dwight," she continued, "after we portage, we will be on which river?"

"The Wisconsin. W-I-S-C-O-N-S-I-N," Dwight answered.

Jane now knew that to portage meant to carry boats and luggage overland from one body of water to another. They had already portaged once.

"And the last river?" Lucy challenged Evert.

"The Mississippi," he said. "How do you

spell that, Cousin Lucy?"

"M-I-S-S-I-S-S-I-P-P-I," and she reeled off the letters expertly. Jane began counting on her fingers the number of letters Lucy had said. Lucy went on, "The place where the Fox and Wisconsin Rivers are closest is where we will stop and go by wagon from one river to the other. This portage has a fort, Fort Winnebago. It is an unusual place, a 'continental divide,' because the Fox River runs north, and the Wisconsin River runs south."

A shrill whistle interrupted them. All the diners rushed to look out. Wedged between adults, Jane saw log houses coming into view.

"And it looks as if we about to portage," Lucy said cheerfully.

Throughout the bustle of unloading the boat, Jane stayed close to Mrs. Stevens, who sighed wearily from time to time. Two wagons arrived, and people and luggage were piled into them. The passengers joked and tried to make themselves comfortable on their trunks and boxes, for the wagons had seats only for the drivers.

The road was merely a path through marshy land. The wagons bumped and jostled along slowly. The passengers grasped the sides, and Sarah held on tightly to Jane after she had fallen from her perch twice, landing on Dr. Williamson's feet.

It was only about two miles, the driver said, but everyone seemed glad when the white walls of Fort Winnebago came into view, standing on a hill above the river. The road ended there. They had a welcome dinner of boiled pork, biscuits, plum cake, and coffee. The room was so new it still smelled of pine from its walls and tables.

It rained during the night, but the sun was out in the early morning when their next boat awaited them on the Wisconsin River. Shouts and laughter from the landing caused Jane to look toward where Dwight and Evert were playing happily. She saw the reverend peering at the boys, frowning.

A boatman came up to him. Jane shuddered at his rough-looking face, but his voice was gentle. "Let them play, sir. We don't see many children here. Let them have their fun. I will get my men to help with the baggage."

Once again they headed out onto a river. On land, everything was washed fresh after the rain, and the spring sun made diamonds on the water. At first there were grasslands with oaks here and there, but then the forest grew heavier again.

Everyone was quiet, except when the mosqui-

toes were irritating. There were mumbles and com-
plaints then, and slapping of the insects. Then it
became quiet again.

Once, Evert pointed out a place to Jane where
two small islands created a pond between the shore
and the river. "That would make a great place to
skate in the winter," he said.

Jane nodded, keeping her eyes on the little
pond until she could no longer see it.

The boat rounded a bend and a village came
into view. The passengers stood up thankfully to
peer ahead.

"It is May 22, 1835, and we have arrived at
Prairie du Chien," said the reverend. "Thank the
Lord."

"Amen!" said Dr. Williamson.

Jane looked up at him curiously. She liked his
enthusiasm.

The boat stopped. Men came running from
the long, low buildings near the shore. Quickly they
unloaded the boat, piling bags and trunks onto
wheelbarrows. The passengers headed to the nearest
boarding house, one that faced the great Mississippi
River.

Jane, swinging Mrs. Stevens's hat box, joined

the boys as they skipped along.

"There it is!" Dwight said. "The M-I-S-S-I-S-S-I-P-P-I!"

Evert and Jane copied, "M-I-S-S-I-S-S-I-P-P-I!"

"Stop that, children," said the reverend. His voice sounded weary. "You are showing off. 'The foolish shall not stand in thy sight'."

They ate supper in the crowded dining room, and when darkness approached, the tall, thin woman who had served their supper began showing people to their rooms. Lucy took Jane's hand, and with Miss Sarah they climbed the narrow stairway after the woman, who carried a candle. The little flame feebly lit the unfamiliar way. Opening a door near the top of the stairs, the woman led them inside.

"I am sorry, ladies, but this will have to do. There is only one bed," she said, dipping the candle to light a smaller one on the dresser. With her hand on a bolt on the door, she added, "The door fastens this way. Good night."

Lucy locked it behind her, and the three turned to look at the room in the soft light. Sarah looked as if she were about to cry. Lucy laughed merrily and said, "We can sleep crosswise! Jane, you will be fine, but Sarah and I will have to curl up a bit!"

Jane nestled into the bed as Lucy and Sarah

tried to make themselves comfortable. She heard Sarah give a sigh in the darkness, and then Jane slept.

At breakfast the next morning, Jane listened to the words of the boardinghouse keeper who paused at their table.

"Pardon me, ma'am, for being so bold, but upriver, into Sioux country, is no place for ladies and a little girl," he said gently to Mrs. Stevens.

She nodded uncomfortably, then said, "Yes, but we are here to do God's work."

"You really ought to be going downstream, not into Sioux country," he urged.

"Thank you for your concern," Lucy said stoutly. "And we appreciate your fine food."

"Thank you, miss," he said, and left the table.

Jane looked out the window. The Mississippi River lay smooth under the early morning sky. No place for a little girl? If there wasn't any place for her, where would she sleep?

Six days later, a small steamboat, "The Otter," came into view. There was the usual scurrying for baggage, but soon the whole party was aboard.

The boardinghouse keeper came to the dock to wave good-bye. He still wore a troubled look. Jane wondered if the reverend could stay here in Prairie du Chien to do his work. It had such a pretty name, and here at least there was a place for her, even if she had to sleep crosswise on a bed.

Evert, however, was bubbling over with excitement. "This is the last part of the river journey!" he said to Jane. "This boat goes up to Fort Snelling only twice a year! Look, Jane, see those soldiers? They are on their way to the fort. That is where we are going to stay! At the fort!"

She looked at the soldiers' smart uniforms, and saw Dwight eyeing these men, too. He and Evert would be glad to stay at a fort, instead of just seeing it, like Fort Crawford at Prairie du Chien.

Miss Sarah was looking forlornly out of the boat, and Mrs. Williamson put her hand on her shoulder. Jane heard her say, "Do not be sad, Sarah. This is a new field. We are needed in Sioux country."

The reverend said to his wife, "At last we are nearing the field of our labors!" Then he began pacing slowly up and down the deck. Mrs. Stevens sat contentedly with her knitting.

Field? Jane wondered if they intended to farm. But the scenery was changing. There was much to see.

"Look, Evert!" Jane said, pointing to huge bluffs rising along the river bank. They were varying shades of green, as trees covered them.

Dr. Williamson had joined Reverend Stevens now. The reverend said, "Two years ago, when I came this way, there was an Indian village some-where along here. Their chief was Wabasha. Oh, look! It is still there!"

Jane gazed at the shoreline. She could see something that looked like tents.

"If you passed through here two years ago, you were here not long after the Battle of the Bad Axe," Dr. Williamson said.

The reverend nodded. "That was north of here, near a bluff supposedly four hundred feet high! I understand it was terrible, hundreds of starving Sac and Fox Indians killed—"

Dr. Williamson touched the reverend's arm and nodded toward Jane and Evert, who were listen-ing intently. The two men turned, and walked away.

Jane sat silently, feeling the grace and beauty

of this magnificent place, but wondering why there was sadness here, too.

She woke up in the night to realize the boat had stopped. The sound of the waves lulled her back to sleep easily, but only moments later, it seemed, she heard Mrs. Stevens say, "Wake up, child! We will leave the boat very soon."

As she hurriedly fastened Jane's dress, Jane asked sleepily, "Where are we?"

"We are at Fort Snelling," Mrs. Stevens said. "Hurry now."

When they reached the deck, Jane saw a steep bluff crowned by long stone buildings and watch towers. Cannons peered out from the fort walls.

The captain approached Dr. Williamson and Reverend Stevens. He informed them, "The army wagons are coming down to get the supplies we have carried. There will be a wagon reserved for

your people."

Jane, Dwight, and Evert watched together as the wagons lumbered down the long hill.

"They are pulled by mules—mules!—not horses!" Jane squealed.

"I like all the soldiers," Dwight said, standing straight, as if he held a sword by his side. "When I grow up, I am going to be a soldier. Look at those uniforms! I want to wear a proud hat like that!"

Evert said, "See how tall that watch tower is? And look at all the holes in the walls—loopholes—where the cannons poke out."

The wagons had drawn up now, and the unloading and reloading of supplies and baggage began.

The reverend looked up and said quietly to Mrs. Stevens, "We have finally arrived! Seven weeks after leaving Fort Mackinac, we have come to Fort Snelling."

She nodded. "And a year since we left New York."

A year. Jane knew that was a long, long time. It was now a long, long time since she had been home.

The soldier who drove their wagon was now welcoming them. "There is much to see and do here!" he said cheerfully. "We are a military outpost, so you will see plenty of soldiers and plenty of horses, and plenty of guns. Also, the fur depot is nearby. And, of course, there are parties and dances!"

Miss Sarah and Lucy exchanged happy glances. Dwight and Evert grinned at each other. Jane sat up straight, looking ahead to the fort as the mules strained to pull the wagon up the bluff.

After long months of quiet traveling, the activity and noise at Fort Snelling were fascinating. Everywhere she looked, Jane found something to see. Outside one long building, two women scrubbed clothes in washtubs, talking as they worked. From the stables came the whinnying of horses. Uniformed men stood in pairs, speaking and gesturing. A few children ran, shouted, skipped. Jane smelled the tallow that was being made into candles. She surveyed the warm, rich colors of the wool blankets in the sutler's store. The large flag snapped and flapped proudly over the most beautiful building, the commandant's house. People called to each other in greeting. Fur traders walked by, speaking in French.

She awoke each dawn to the sound of trumpets as the soldiers lined up outside in the huge, open area called the parade grounds. The sun would be rising over the bluffs, streaking the sky with a shy pink, when the clatter of boots, shouts of orders, and general shuffle filled the air. Jane and Evert watched out the window of their quarters. About eight-thirty,

they could count on seeing a few sick soldiers being carried from their barracks to the hospital. At nine o'clock, there was another roll call just before breakfast. The work of the day started, and Jane saw soldiers sweeping the parade grounds. It took a long time, and she knew they were bored. Bored also by watching them, she began wandering.

The laundresses were friendly, and she smelled the soap as she neared them. The aroma made her vaguely remember someone, but she was not sure who it was. She noticed how red and chapped their hands were, but they were cheerful as they talked with each other.

One day she paused to watch the soldiers who were working as carpenters. She sifted the fine sawdust between her fingers. It was soft and gritty at the same time.

"My papa is a carpenter," she shyly told one soldier.

He looked up, hammer in hand. "I thought your pa was a preacher."

"No, that is Reverend Stevens. He is not my papa," Jane said.

The soldier nodded uncertainly, and went back to his work.

At three o'clock, there was a third roll call. After supper, just before sunset, everyone watched the troops, clad smartly in dress uniforms, as they

marched around in straight rows, their boots sometimes stirring up dust.

Dwight stood
with her. She
knew how
he

loved to
watch the soldiers.
He said one evening,
"See how smart those white
trousers look with the black
boots. I like the way the jackets are short in front,
and long in back."

"I like the things on their shoulders," Jane
said. "They make the uniform pretty."

"Pretty?" Dwight scoffed. "Those are the
epaulets. They show the soldier's rank!"

Jane shrugged. "They are still pretty. But their

collars look horrible! They are so stiff and tall, I think they would be very uncomfortable!" She put her hands around her neck, and stuck out her tongue as if she were choking.

"A soldier's life is not meant to be comfortable," Dwight said, as though he thought that was wonderful.

A shrill call on a bugle caused the company to change directions.

"I am trying to learn each bugle call," Dwight said.

Jane did not answer. She was watching the horses instead. She loved their high, mincing steps. They looked so noble in line, like soldiers themselves. All too soon the horses were led into the stables, and the fort quieted down for the night.

There were not many women at Fort Snelling, so the arrival of Mrs. Stevens, Mrs. Williams, Lucy, and Sarah was cause for much visiting. Despite the roughness of the land around them, the women wore silk dresses that seemed to whisper, and they spoke in soft voices. They referred to Jane as "Mrs. Stevens's little girl," and Jane did not correct them. She was not sure of what to say.

Mrs. Clark was Jane's favorite. She would

draw Jane close to her, as Mrs. Stevens never did. Jane liked the feel of her billowing skirt, and the softness of her hand on Jane's hand.

One day she arrived at the Stevenses' quarters with a book.

"I have brought you a gift, Jane. My daughter Charlotte is a great big girl now, and she does not read Mother Goose stories anymore. I would like you to have her book," she said, her kind face in a smile.

"Oh, thank you! Thank you! My own book!" Jane exclaimed, her eyes shining.

She smiled up at Mrs. Clark, then glanced at Mrs. Stevens who hastily wiped her eyes.

"I will take good care of it!" Jane went on.

"I am sure you will," Mrs. Clark said. "I am glad it has found a good home!"

It was while she was reading this book one day that the reverend burst in, his face contorted with anger.

"I will not have it!" he stormed in a voice that frightened Jane. "That scoundrel Williamson wants the land by Lake Calhoun for his mission!"

"Dr. Williamson? Our friend?" Mrs. Stevens asked.

"Friend? Friend! I was here once before, I

have seen it! That is my mission! The scoundrel!"

"He is good man," Mrs. Stevens ventured carefully.

The reverend looked at her, his eyes narrow, but Jane knew he wasn't really seeing her. "He seems religious enough, but is he zealous? People who are merely religious but not zealous are worse than those who are unreligious, Julia!"

"He has done much good for others, don't you think, Jedediah?" she ventured timidly.

"Yes, but he is far from perfect."

Uncertainly, Mrs. Stevens answered, "Well, yes...."

With a wave of his hand, the reverend said, "Besides, I am certain the Lord wants me to have this mission. How could it be any other way?"

Mrs. Stevens nodded quickly. "Perhaps God is calling him to an even more remote area. Mrs. Williamson has spoken of his medical skills. Here there is a doctor already."

Looking at her now, the reverend said more calmly, "Perhaps! Let us hope he finds it in his heart to do what is right! After all, he may be a doctor, but he is not ordained, as I am."

Jane closed her book, watching and listening. She noticed that the reverend's jaw looked as if it were made of stone.

"Cousin Lucy, what does the word 'zealous' mean?" Jane asked.

Lucy cocked her head as if it helped her to think. "Enthusiastic. Intense. Earnest. Why do you want to know, Jane?"

"Because the reverend said Dr. Williamson was not zealous."

"Oh," Lucy said. "Well, Jane, Uncle Jed and Dr. Williamson were having a disagreement. But it has been all worked out. The Indian agent, Major Taliaferro, has told Dr. Williamson that he is needed at a mission about two hundred miles from here. He and Mrs. Williamson and Sarah will move there, and we will go to Lake Calhoun, which is not nearly so far from here. Only a few miles. Now, would you like to go for a walk with me? It is a fine evening."

Jane and Lucy strolled in the lingering sunlight. They climbed into one of the fort's lookouts. Jane saw below them the swallows darting in and out of the holes in the wall.

"Two rivers come together here, Jane," Lucy said.

"We have seen so many rivers!" Jane answered.

"Rivers are important. They bring people

from one place to another. They bring needed supplies so the people can live. Of course they can take people away, too. I have heard of drownings here, but then people could drown back home, too. Mostly, life in the wilderness is better than I imagined. At least here at the fort, for me. But then I am not a soldier or a laundress," Lucy said, pausing to watch a bird in the distance. "Uncle Jed will leave soon. He will go to Lake Calhoun and begin to build the Mission House. We will stay here until it is finished. He will come back here on weekends to preach."

"Does the reverend know how to build a house?" Jane asked, surprised.

"Well, I guess so," Lucy said, but her voice seemed to lose some of its usual certainly. "Jane, you do not need to call him 'the reverend.' You could call him 'Uncle Jed' or even 'Father'."

Jane rubbed her fingers over the thick limestone wall and gazed out over the two rivers. She did not answer.

Jane did not miss the reverend. One night she attended a play. The actors were officers at the fort, and some played women's parts. Jane recognized one of Mrs. Clark's shawls on the shoulders of an actor.

There were tea parties. Some adults played cards and dominoes, and there was even a small library that Lucy and Miss Sarah visited.

Major Taliaferro

One warm Sunday afternoon, Jane sat outside with Miss Sarah and Cousin Lucy. They noticed a tall, lanky man walking across the parade grounds, on his way to the commandant's house.

"That is Major Taliaferro," Lucy said.

"Oh?" Miss Sarah said, interested. "I have heard so much about him!"

"He is the Indian agent, and is so good at it that he has been asked for many years to continue his job. He is supposed to help the Indian people here. He believes they must leave hunting behind and take up farming," Lucy said.

"He is quite handsome," Sarah observed. "Mrs. Clark says he has intent but gentle eyes."

"They say some call him 'Four Hearts' because he always tries to be fair to everyone—the Indians, the French, the Americans, everyone."

Sarah laughed. "My sister told me she heard a Sioux chief called him 'No-Sugar-in-Your-Mouth' because he never makes promises he can't keep, and he always talks honestly."

"Both are very honorable names," Lucy said. "Do you wonder, Sarah, when we leave here, if we shall be seen as being so admirable in our work?"

Sarah pulled her shawl a little closer around her shoulders. "I do not like to think about leaving here, Lucy. We will be so far away from anyone else!"

Both of the young women now were silent, and Jane sensed their sadness and fear. Where was this place they would go to? This place where the reverend who couldn't build was building a house?

And would there be room for her?

Major Taliaferro stretched his long legs under the table. The reverend sat forward eagerly, and Mrs. Stevens sat politely with her hands in her lap.

Dwight and Evert had been shooed out of the quarters into the August heat, but Jane, in a corner with her book, had been allowed to stay. Shyly, she peeked at the man called "Four Hearts." Yes, he had kind eyes, and Jane liked his long nose.

"I am glad you get along so well with Samuel and Gideon Pond," the major said to Reverend Stevens. "They are amongst the finest of men, I think."

"Yes," the reverend agreed. "They are superb carpenters. The progress on our Mission House is remarkable, thanks to their skills. They are truly pious, very dedicated to saving souls. They will be a great help to my work there. I am impressed, too, with how much of the Sioux language they speak."

"They are truly remarkable with languages! Even before they arrived here, those brothers from Connecticut had begun to learn Dakota—most whites call them Sioux, but the Indians prefer 'Dakota.' It is a difficult language, but Samuel and Gideon have put out great effort to learn it, and have even begun to write it by using the English alphabet."

Jane remembered the children on Mackinac Island. Were there children at Lake Calhoun, too? And did they speak English, or French, or Dakota? She did not ask out loud.

"Back home, the Ponds took part in a revival, and it changed them forever. They both decided to devote their lives to spreading God's word. As they traveled west, they learned of the Dakota people and became determined to seek them out. They arrived here at the fort with the backing of no church, but determined to be missionaries. Their talents, I think, lie best in learning languages. We can make very little progress if there is a language barrier."

The reverend nodded absently. Mrs. Stevens made no movement.

"But they also have farming skills, something desperately needed here. They both have been successful in teaching different Indian groups how to plow. Samuel even had a plow floated downstream to one village."

"The Sioux—Dakota—do not know how to plow?" said a voice so shy, so tentative, it was barely heard. It was Mrs. Stevens.

Major Taliaferro smiled warmly at her. "No, ma'am, they have not had the opportunity to own plows. They live mainly by hunting and gathering, mostly nuts and berries in the woods and wild rice and cranberries in the streams and marshes. They work hard—very hard—to feed their children. Both the men and women spend most of their time providing for their families. They are an ambitious people, but times are changing, and there will be more and more settlement of white people here. What is now a hard and demanding way to live will soon become impossible. I am trying to help them learn farming. It is, perhaps, their only salvation."

"And hearing the word of God," the reverend said.

The major said, "Certainly. I am grateful for your presence and your work, and I truly believe God's work is at the heart of this, but we must keep in mind that hungry stomachs cannot listen very well."

Jane stirred on her chair.

"I have great hopes for Eatonville, which is what I call the village near Lake Calhoun and Lake Harriet. Have you met Chief Cloud Man?"

The reverend nodded, and shrugged. "Yes, Samuel introduced me. We could not speak to each other, of course."

"A man of great integrity. He wants the best

for his people, and he has much foresight. Cloud Man was a war chief, and is, of course, a hunter. I had talked with him some time ago about pursuing farming. There is planting of corn and some other vegetables each year, but the main source of food is the hunt. Well, one recent winter, he and his men were caught in a terrible blizzard, which out on a prairie is almost certain death. He decided then that if he and any of his men survived, he would take up my farming ideas. He did live through it, and now, with the help of the Pond brothers, what started as an experiment with a few men is a village with fourteen bark lodges, each with two or three families. Not all of Cloud Man's people agreed to farm, and those who did not moved to another village. But last year, his current village had thirty—thirty!—acres under cultivation. The yield was about eight hundred bushels!"

"My goodness!" Mrs. Stevens exclaimed.

"It will be an interesting life, Mrs. Stevens. I wish you the best," said the major gently. Then, turning to Jane, he added, "And you, little lady, will have many playmates!"

September had begun to touch the tree tops. Standing on the lookout at Fort Snelling, Jane could see miles of green mixed with hints of orange, red, yellow, and brown.

The air was cooler now, and when the reverend returned on weekends to preach he said the work on the Mission House was nearly complete, thanks to the Pond brothers. He was very glad, for during the week he slept in a tent near the house, and it was getting cold at night.

Jane awoke one morning to the familiar sound of the bugles. Sitting up in her bed she saw that the trunks and carpet bags were out and open.

"Jane," Mrs. Stevens said in a distracted manner, "Get dressed. Then put your good dress and other aprons in the trunk. And your book. We are leaving for Lake Harriet tomorrow."

Sitting on the edge of her bed, Jane noticed how heavy and tired Mrs. Stevens looked.

As Lucy tied Jane's apron strings, Jane said, "I thought we were going to Lake Calhoun. Why did Mrs. Stevens say Lake Harriet?"

"They are near each other," Lucy said, beginning to brush her own long hair up into a bun. "The Pond brothers have a small cabin on Lake Calhoun. Our Mission House is on the other lake, Lake Harriet. That is where we will live, and I will teach school."

The following morning, Jane said good-bye to her friend Mrs. Clark. Miss Sarah wept openly as she and Lucy embraced, Mrs. Stevens and Mrs. Williamson kissed each other's cheeks, and Reverend Stevens and Dr. Williamson shook hands stiffly.

Their many friends patted Jane on her head, telling her to be good. The trunks and bags were loaded into a wagon. Mrs. Stevens adjusted her bonnet, and the family climbed into the wagon. Amongst cheerful shouts of "good-bye" and "good luck," the wagon started off on its way to the Dakota village that was to be Jane's new home.

Turtle Soup

Chapter Four

"We are coming to a hill, children," the reverend said, "You may alight, climb the hill, and tell us what you see."

As Dwight, Evert, and Jane gleefully jumped from the wagon, Mrs. Stevens said, "Lucy, please go with them. I am too tired to climb."

They scrambled up the hill, through hazel-brush and rose briars that snagged on Jane's skirt.

All day they had been traveling on a path never meant for wagons. As they were bumped and jostled unendingly, the reverend explained that this was an Indian trail, one the Dakota took to Fort Snelling and the trading post there.

They stopped only once, to water the horses and eat near a sparkling stream called the "Little River." Lucy said she had heard there was a magnificent waterfall on this stream, but it was too far out of their way to travel there today.

No one minded, especially Mrs. Stevens. Cousin Lucy kept asking her how she was feeling. From time to time Mrs. Stevens put her hand to the small of her back or ran her hand lightly over her belly, which, Jane noted, was much larger than it had ever been before.

"A path!" Evert announced. The others followed him to the top of the hill where something white caught Jane's eye. It was cloth, tied to a pole. Other poles nearby also had cloths tied to them. These poles supported small platforms on which bundles were securely tied. Small piles of food lay at the feet of some of the poles.

Lucy put her hand on Jane's shoulder, and spoke softly into the prairie wind. "The burial ground. I suppose when the ground freezes one can-

not dig a grave, so these platforms are used until the ground thaws. Look, someone has left food for her loved one."

Dwight ran up, shouting, "Look! Look farther ahead. You can see the village and the lakes!"

They all gazed down to where a cluster of long houses of bark stood together, surrounded by cornfields mellow in the afternoon sun. Jane saw small fires with smoke drifting lazily upward, and people tending them. Beyond them lay the lakes. A large, new, wooden house stood proudly on the banks of one lake.

"Our new house," Lucy said, pointing. Then, with a sweep of her hand, she added, "Our new life."

The children gladly walked as the wagon lumbered toward the village. Jane trudged along as quickly as her short legs could carry her, trying to keep up with Dwight and Evert.

Suddenly, the silence of the great prairie was pierced by laughter and shouts as Dakota children came running from all directions. Their dogs came with them and Jane was surrounded by jumping, yelping dogs, and by children with curious, smiling faces.

Boys and girls pressed close to her and Dwight and Evert. They were eager to talk, and Jane listened just as eagerly. She did not understand any of their words, but their happy faces and excited eyes told her she was among friends.

As the wagon creaked to a halt behind them, two young white men came running up. Both were tall. Jane looked up into two kind faces.

"Welcome!" one of them said.

"Mr. Stevens! Welcome back! And welcome to your family, too!" the other man said.

The reverend jumped down from the wagon.

"Thank you. Mr. Samuel Pond, Mr. Gideon Pond, this is my wife, and my niece," the reverend said, pushing a dog away.

The dogs continued to yelp and jump at the wagon. The young man named Samuel turned to the Dakota children, and said something Jane could not understand. She did understand the gentleness in his voice.

"I am pleased to meet you, Mrs. Stevens," Samuel said pleasantly in English. "And Miss Stevens."

Jane saw him noticing Mrs. Stevens' heaviness.

"Please allow us to assist you, Mrs. Stevens, in getting settled into your new home," he offered.

"Why, yes, thank you very much," she answered.

"And these are your children?" Samuel asked.

The reverend nodded. "My sons, Dwight and Evert. And this is Jane."

Jane felt a soft touch on her blonde braid. A Dakota girl, smaller than Jane, was shyly fingering Jane's hair. Jane admired the other girl's black hair. Lucy noticed and laughed.

"And are these my pupils?" she asked, indicating the Dakota children.

"Perhaps, if they can be enticed. But then, aren't we all learners?" Samuel said.

Lucy looked at him, puzzled.

"You will find them a curious, happy group

of children, Miss Stevens," he added.

The little girl let Jane's braid slip from her fingers. Jane smiled at her and was rewarded with a big grin.

"My brother and I will unload the wagon with the help of the children," Gideon suggested.

In Dakota, he spoke to the other children and they moved closer to the wagon, ready to help.

"You speak Sioux, Mr. Pond," Dwight ventured.

Gideon gave him an easy smile. "Yes, I speak Dakota, and I have a feeling you will, too."

Mrs. Stevens and Lucy began unpacking at once.

"Jane! Dwight! Evert!" called Mrs. Stevens. "You are needed inside now!"

All three came in reluctantly, for the Dakota children were still talking with Samuel and Gideon, and Jane paused in the doorway. The girl who had admired her braids looked back at her.

"Jane!" Mrs. Stevens demanded sharply. "If you do not come this instant, you will be sorry!"

Jane hastened into the house, but not before she saw Samuel glance at her, and then say something to the other children. They began walking back towards their homes.

"Unpack these dishes," Mrs. Stevens said wearily. "Next time you do not come when you are called, I will take a switch to you!"

There was a knock at the door. Samuel and Gideon stood there.

"Ma'am, we have taken the liberty of bringing some cornbread and buffalo meat for your dinner," Gideon said, indicating a basket he carried.

"Thank you very much," Mrs. Stevens said. "You have been so helpful to us already."

Lucy exclaimed impulsively, "How lovely! Shall we have supper all together?"

And so they feasted on their first night. Jane wasn't sure she liked buffalo meat, but she was certain she liked the Pond brothers. She sat quietly, hoping to be allowed to stay up late and listen to the conversation.

"The house is beautiful," Lucy said, gesturing to the walls made of tamarack logs.

"Yes, we are most grateful for your skills as a carpenter," the reverend said to Gideon.

Gideon shrugged. "It is the Dakotas' interest in Jesus that I would like to build," he said simply.

"You have a good start, with how much Sioux—or Dakota—you speak," Lucy said.

Samuel grinned. "We never miss a chance to

learn more words. It is a difficult but fascinating language. I am working on a dictionary right now, so I carry a bottle of ink with me at all times," he said, patting a small bag at his side. "When I learn a new word, I write it down."

"Do the Sioux look strangely at you when you write down their words?" Lucy asked.

"No, they are used to me and my ways by now," Samuel said with a chuckle.

"Actually, the funniest reaction we ever got was when we were traveling here. We stopped, of course, in Prairie du Chien," Gideon said. "Several Dakota men were bartering with white traders there. Samuel asked the trader how to ask in Dakota the name of an object. Then he went around the store asking Dakota men the names of the merchandise in the store. He wrote down each word. Both the Dakota and traders looked at us strangely that day!"

The reverend gave a little grunt. Mrs. Stevens looked at him nervously.

"It was a good start, though," Samuel said. "A very good start."

"Tell me about the girls here," Lucy said. "Will they come to school, or will they only send their boys?"

"They may not send anyone, Miss Stevens,"

Gideon said. "Dakota parents and grandparents teach the children themselves everything that is needed for survival."

"They do not wish their children to learn to read and write?" asked Mrs. Stevens.

"They are an ignorant people," the reverend said.

"I have not found that to be true, sir," Samuel said. "They know a great deal of which we are ignorant."

Jane saw the reverend shift uneasily in his chair. Lucy did, too.

"We will hold school, won't we?" Lucy asked.

"Of course," the reverend said. "Mr. Pond has agreed to help us build a school building."

Gideon nodded.

"I will find a way to get the children into the school," Lucy said, looking determined.

"I am sure you will, Miss Stevens. I have teaching experience, too. If you are successful in getting a large number of children, I can join you. And now my brother and I must go home and let you rest," Samuel said, rising. Gideon joined him.

Suddenly Mrs. Stevens looked confused. "Your home? Do you live in one of the bark lodges?"

"No, ma'am," Gideon said. "We have a cabin

on the other lake, on Lake Calhoun, about a mile from here."

As the door closed upon them, Jane heard the reverend say, "How can this house be the center of mission activity when they live a mile away?"

Jane felt her way through the darkness of the September night to the bedroom she would share with Lucy. Lying in bed, she could hear distant singing coming from the village. She wondered which of the bark lodges the Dakota children were in, and if they were sleepy, too.

"Uncle Jed, did you worry about this Mission House not being the center of activity? You can put your mind to rest on that!" Lucy said, with a laugh.

The door had just closed for the tenth time that first day, and it was not yet supper time. All day, there had been a steady stream of visitors, Dakota men and women who had come to welcome the new family and to satisfy their curiosity about them.

The first visitors had been two women and a baby. Jane thought they were mother, daughter, and granddaughter. They entered the house quietly and sat just as quietly on the floor, their legs drawn up under them to the right side. Jane tried to sit like them, but after a few minutes, her ankles ached.

They wore blue skirts and leggings, both of a cotton cloth that Jane thought she had seen at Fort Snelling. It was a cool day, so each had heavy blankets for coats. Each woman wore her long hair in neat braids.

Shy Mrs. Stevens tried to be gracious to these women she thought were so different from herself,

but she could only sit on a chair and smile nervously.

Lucy came to the rescue. She greatly admired the hand-work on the younger woman's blanket and skirt. Several colors of bright ribbons had been carefully sewn onto the blanket in a pattern that Lucy exclaimed over.

"There must be a foot of embroidery around this skirt! It is lovely!" Lucy said, and her sincerity was not lost for lack of language.

Mrs. Stevens's knitting basket sat near the fireplace. The younger Dakota woman carefully examined the half-finished sock. Jane watched her fingering it, peering at the stitches. She smiled shyly at Lucy, returning the basket to exactly where it had been.

There was silence again. Then the younger woman pointed to Jane, saying something in Dakota. When Mrs. Stevens and Lucy did not understand, the older woman pointed to the chubby baby on her lap. Jane had been admiring the tiny girl with the sparkling black eyes. Happily, she fingered the beads around her grandmother's neck. The grandmother patted the baby, saying, "We-harka."

She then pointed to Mrs. Stevens, smiling, and saying something in Dakota.

"Aunt Julia, I think she is asking when your

baby is due," Lucy said quietly.

Jane started. Baby? Mrs. Stevens? Then she saw Mrs. Stevens's face go very red.

Lucy turned to the grandmother. "Winter," she explained, then to herself uttered, "Oh, I wish I could speak Sioux!"

Jane jumped up. A baby in winter? No one had told her. But someone must answer this question. She hugged herself, shivering, then holding out her arms, made her fingers wiggle to indicate snow falling.

The visitors understood. Both smiled at Mrs. Stevens, for they knew the difficulties and joys of babies, especially babies born in the winter. Then they stood, and with We-harka cooing at Jane, quickly left.

Mrs. Stevens sank back in her chair, but Lucy paced the floor. "I must talk with Mr. Pond about learning this language!" she said, almost fiercely.

The visiting had gone on like that all day, sometimes men arriving to visit with the reverend, other times more women. The reverend was greatly pleased by all the attention.

"It is a good sign, Julia! You must continue to be welcoming to them. You will be a good example to them, you a God-fearing, respectable woman!" he said enthusiastically, pacing the floor and waving his arms in a way that made Jane think of his preaching. "You and Lucy must always show them how Christian women should act. It is your duty, as mine is to convert them by my words."

Mrs. Stevens sighed. Jane thought of the gentle grandmother with the baby in her arms.

As Dwight came in with firewood, the Pond brothers stopped by, their tall presence seeming to bring a light into the room.

"I hear you have received many visitors," Gideon said. "And Mrs. Stevens, your knitting seems to be the talk among some of the women. Perhaps you will be asked to teach it!"

"Speaking of teaching, Mr. Pond," the reverend said. "When do you expect to begin the school building?"

"Tomorrow, for I will be needing help from others, and I hope to have as much done as possible before most everyone leaves for the hunt."

"The hunt?" Lucy asked.

"The corn harvest is almost in, so soon it will be time for the families to move to hunting grounds. Some gather wild foods, others hunt. Almost everyone goes. The whole village moves, for they take their homes with them. These bark lodges stay here, of course, but they take their tipi, the skin tents, and set up camp where hunting or gathering is best."

"But they cannot go!" the reverend said, rising from his chair. "How will I do my work?"

Gideon said quietly, "They must eat, and feed their children."

"Yes, but they are farmers now," Lucy said stoutly.

"The Dakota people are experimenting with farming, Miss Stevens. They had a good harvest of corn this year, but they cannot live just on that. They must hunt if they are to have meat in their diet."

"I have spoken with Chief Cloud Man," Samuel said. "Usually most of a village moves to another location for the winter, then to a sugar camp for maple sugar in March. They come back to the summer village in late spring. But as these people are experimenting with a new way of life, Chief Cloud Man thinks that after the hunt at least some of them will return here. They will set up their skin tents, however, for the bark lodges are pleasant in the warm months, but would never be sufficient in the winter."

Lucy frowned. "All this moving around. It does not seem practical to me! What a way to live!"

"Miss Stevens, scripture tells us, 'God put no

difference between us and them'," Gideon said, smiling warmly at her.

Jane had just finished putting away the last of the breakfast dishes when the reverend called to her to come into his small study. What had she done wrong? Jane wondered as she entered, wiping her hands on her apron.

He glanced up. "Go to the Ponds' house and tell Mr. Gideon Pond I want to see him right away," the reverend said, then went back to reading the Bible on the table before him.

Jane hesitated. She had no idea where the Pond cabin was.

He looked up again.

"Go!"

Jane fled, grabbing her shawl from a peg as she went.

The morning sun was softly touching the golden grasses as Jane stepped out into the cool air. Lake Harriet looked cold but beautiful. Only a short distance away stood the bark lodges of the Dakota people. They would know where to find Mr. Pond, if she could find a way to ask.

Her bare feet felt the autumn cold in the ground as she neared the first lodge. Smells of cooking filled the air, and a few dogs ran up to greet her. Then a woman came out of a lodge. She was beautiful and very graceful. She approached Jane, patted Jane's head, then touched her own chest, saying, "Wakaninajinwin."

She is telling me her name, Jane thought, and so repeated slowly, "Wakaninajinwin." Then, Jane pointed to herself and said, "Jane."

"Jane," the woman said, smiling, and gesturing for Jane to come into her home.

Jane shook her head, thinking of the reverend. Instead, she put her hand over her eyebrows, as if she was looking for someone. Jane reached up as tall as she could, and said, "Pond."

Wakaninajinwin nodded, then stepped inside her house. In a moment, she came out with a little girl younger than Jane. The child looked up at Jane and for a moment, Jane could not take her eyes away. She was the prettiest little girl Jane had ever seen. She was fairly certain this was the child who had shyly touched Jane's hair when they had first arrived.

Wakaninajinwin said, "Jane. Winona." This was Wakaninajinwin's daughter, and she would take Jane to the Ponds' house.

Winona grasped Jane's hand and the two girls walked through the cornfields toward Lake Calhoun.

Jane noticed posts with platforms like those in the graveyard. On a few of these sat women or girls. Jane paused to look.

Some of the corn was still in the field, and when a flock of blackbirds descended, the women

closest to the flock leaped to their feet, shouting and clapping. The birds flew away.

Jane turned to Winona in amazement.

"They are here to scare the birds away?" Jane asked, forgetting Winona did not speak English.

But Winona seemed to understand. She gave a merry laugh, then she pointed to herself and to a platform not far away. Soon she must take her turn.

As they neared the lake, Jane saw a small, snug cabin. Smoke rose from its chimney. Winona pointed, smiled, and then ran towards the cornfield. Jane approached the cabin.

A tall Dakota man was standing at the door of the cabin, talking with Gideon Pond. Jane admired the man's white blanket that served as his coat. When he left, Gideon saw her.

"Hello, Miss Jane! Come in!" he said.

"Hello, Mr. Pond." she said shyly. Shouts from the cornfield could be heard.

"You are finding your way around here already."

"The reverend told me to come, and I did not know the way, so I asked in the village."

"Good for you. Whom did you speak with?"

Jane paused, searching her memory. "Winona's mother. Wakaninajinwin."

"Very good, Jane! In English her name means 'Stands Sacred Woman.' 'Winona' means 'first-born daughter' and when she is older, she will be given a new name, one that tells something about her. She is already a very special child," Gideon said, ushering Jane into the cabin.

It was warm and dark inside. Breakfast dishes sat on the table, where Samuel was busy writing with his quill pen. A bottle of ink stood next to him.

"Good morning, Miss Jane," said Samuel kindly. Jane was startled to realize she longed to climb onto his lap. Instead she greeted him politely.

"Speaking of names, what does 'Jane' mean?" Gideon asked.

Jane shrugged. "It is my mother's name."

"Oh," Gideon said, perplexed. "I had thought it was Julia."

"That is Mrs. Stevens's name," Jane said. The brothers exchanged puzzled looks, but Jane did not notice as she looked about the cabin. She liked it here, very much.

"What did Beaver want?" Samuel asked his brother.

"He stopped by to say that later today there will be some games near here."

"Last fall, when games were played, at least

two hundred people came!" Samuel said.

Gideon laughed at the memory. "Yes, but the winter seems to be coming early, so I do not think the crowd will be so large this year."

"Well," said Samuel. "We have had enough visitors today for a game! Spotted Eagle was here to borrow an ax, Chaske was sent to borrow the hatchet, Badger came for the trap he left here, and now we are honored by Miss Jane!"

"The reverend says you are to come to see him at once, Mr. Gideon."

Gideon asked, "Is something wrong at your house?"

"Oh no, sir." Jane suddenly understood that the Pond brothers knew of the baby to come.

The brothers exchanged looks.

"Of course, I will come," Gideon said.

They walked the mile together, Jane trying to keep up with his long strides. Gideon paused to talk with Dakota people they met along the way. He spoke quickly and easily in Dakota.

"My brother and I are greatly honored to have been given names by the people here," he said. "I am 'Red Eagle' and Samuel is 'Grizzly Bear.' I wonder, Miss Jane, if you too will receive a new name."

When they reached the Mission House, the

reverend came out of his study, and glared at Jane. "How long does it take you, child, to run an errand?"

"It is a mile each way, and keep in mind that she did not even know where my cabin was when she left at your request, sir. She did well making inquiries when she does not speak Dakota."

Jane saw that Gideon looked calmly and evenly at the reverend. Uncomfortable, the reverend looked away from him, then said, "Well, then, Mr. Pond, I want to know now when you will begin the work I need done."

Jane slipped from the room.

It was a golden afternoon of soft, warm breezes. Jane was alone, for Evert and Dwight had been put to work on the new schoolhouse. After her chores, Jane had been allowed to run and play.

She wandered toward the sun-dappled lake, wondering if she could go to the village and look for Winona. Mrs. Stevens had not said she could not. Would Winona be allowed to play with her? Would she want to?

Nearing the water's edge, she sat down in the soft, tall grasses, watching some ducks land gracefully on the mirrored surface of the lake.

Then, a few feet way, a boy stood up. Jane drew back, startled. She had not even known he was there.

He grinned at her, motioning for her to come. Jane hesitated. He pointed to the ground near him, but she could not see what he was pointing to. He kept grinning, and Jane laughed a little, drawing closer.

"Waa-bec," he said, pointing to himself. Then he pointed to her. "Jane."

She was amazed he knew her name. "Jane," he said again, and began chatting happily in Dakota. On the ground was a basket, filled with dried corn. Waa-bec was inviting her to a picnic!

Jane and Waa-bec feasted at the water's edge, pointing at the ducks, the clouds, the people in the distance, saying their own words for them. He gave a lopsided grin each time she said her word, and they would both laugh.

They laughed together for a long time.

There continued to be a steady stream of visitors to the Mission House. Jane enjoyed having her chores interrupted from time to time by the arrival of a Dakota man looking for the reverend. Sometimes a young man would come with his face painted in patterns and colors that left Jane staring.

Lucy would poke her, whispering, "Do not gawk so, Jane!"

Still, even Lucy could not help peering at the skunk skins tied around the ankles of two visitors. Samuel had told Jane that it was usually just the young men who wore the face paint and skunk ornaments. "The older men are too practical for that," he said.

But one day there came a visitor who had the entire household staring. They were finishing dinner when a tall young man appeared at the door. He was dressed elaborately, his hair painted and adorned with many feathers and ribbons. When he was seated near the fire, Jane saw Mrs. Stevens's face go white. She looked back at the visitor and she saw why: a large, striped snake came slithering out from amongst the ornaments in his hair. It darted its head back and forth, slid down the man's back, then slithered back up again.

Lucy stifled a small scream, Mrs. Stevens remained white and silent. The reverend moved his chair back a little, and even Dwight and Evert seemed to grow smaller in their chairs. Jane stared in fascination and horror.

The visit did not last long, but they were still speaking of it when Gideon arrived a few hours later.

"Mr. Pond, we had the most frightening visitor today! It was horrible!" Lucy said.

"Who was it? Did he tell you his name?"

"Yes," Lucy said. "I think it was Wasin Zi. He had a snake—a live one!"

Suddenly Gideon threw his head back and laughed. "So he tried the old 'snake-in-the-headdress' trick again! He did that to Samuel and me, too! You must get to know Wasin Zi! He is quite a jokester! In English his name is Yellow Fat. He really knows how to unnerve the newcomers!"

Gideon laughed again. Jane hoped Yellow Fat would visit again soon.

The nights were longer now, and cold, but the days were warm as the Dakota families prepared to leave. Still there was time for play, and every afternoon Jane, Dwight, and Evert were called outside by shy Dakota children.

"Go ahead," Mrs. Stevens said. "Soon it will be too cold to play outside."

As soon as they were away from the adults, the shyness vanished. Waa-bec and little Winona introduced Jane and the Stevens brothers to the others. They all ran and laughed, chasing each other, and knocking each other down. Some shouted in English, some in Dakota, but still, they understood each other.

One day, down near the lake, Waa-bec suddenly skidded to his knees and crept up to the water's edge. When he stood up, a large turtle dangled helplessly from his hands.

Giving his special grin, Waa-bec said something to Winona. Jane thought one word he had said was "home." Winona nodded, and grabbed Jane by the hand.

"Come with me," she said in Dakota.

Jane ran along, suddenly realizing she had understood Winona's words!

Outside Winona's bark lodge, a large hide was stretched across a frame, drying. Winona led her inside. An older woman was there, sewing a pair of moccasins. This, Jane realized, was Winona's grandmother, Canpadutawin. She stroked Jane's blonde hair gently.

Winona spoke quickly, and her grandmother nodded, gesturing toward a small kettle. Jane understood the words, "Be careful."

Winona handed Jane the kettle, took up live coals from the grandmother's fire and placed them into the kettle. Carefully they carried the coals back to the lake where the turtle was ready for cooking.

Waa-bec, Dwight, and Evert had gathered pine chips, and Waa-bec kindled a fire by placing the coals on the chips. Filling the kettle with water, he placed the turtle into the kettle. While it cooked, they played some more.

Then Waa-bec scooped the turtle out, and, blowing on it to cool it, he broke the shell against a nearby rock. Winona found larger pine chips to use as plates as Waa-bec divided the meat among them. Jane and the Stevens boys had watched with interest, but now they must eat, and they were not sure they wanted to.

"You first," Evert said warily to Dwight.

Waa-bec laughed. Winona giggled.

Dwight looked around, not wanting to taste it.

Waa-bec laughed again and heartily took a bite. So did Winona. Jane followed suit.

"It is good! It is very good!" she exclaimed.

Only then did Dwight and Evert eat. They agreed with Jane, and feasted with their new friends.

Too soon they were called home.

At supper, Mrs. Stevens said, "Are you children not hungry?"

Jane sat at the table, smiling. She was full. Life was full and very good.

Every day Jane, Dwight, and Evert played with Waa-bec and Winona. Now they knew other children too—Chaske, Haparm, Harpen, Waska, and Harpstenah. Soon the Dakota children would be leaving, and studies would resume for Dwight, Evert and Jane. Everyone wanted to get in as much play as possible. And the adults, busy with baby clothing or carpentry, did not mind when the Dakota girls came shyly to the door, politely asking for Jane.

One day Winona motioned for them to come

with her to where some boys were playing beyond the cornfields. Speaking Dakota, she said they were playing the Fire-Throwing Game. Dwight, Evert, and Jane exchanged looks.

"Did she say 'fire-throwing'?" Evert asked, as he ran along.

"I think so," Jane said.

"I hope not!" Dwight exclaimed.

"Come on!" Winona said, her black eyes merry, thick braids bouncing on her back as she ran.

Through the harvested cornfields they ran. The platforms were empty now until another growing season.

Winona stopped and pointed. Waa-bec and Haparm were setting fire to piles of brush they had gathered. The boys formed teams, each with a pile, about fifty yards apart. Each boy picked out sticks from these piles, sticks that were aflame. One team moved toward the other team, shouting and carrying their sticks like flags in the wind. When they were close enough, some began hurling sticks at the other team. Fiery sticks flew through the air, the boys yelling and laughing.

"Most of the time," Winona said slowly, so the others could understand her, "one team backs off."

But not today. Both stood their ground, and
soon they were close enough to hit each other.

"Ouch!" Jane said
in empathy.

Winona nodded.

Smoke and
sparks rose in the air.
The yelling and laugh-
ter continued until all
the sticks went out,
and only the thin-
ning smoke was left
of the fiery game.

Soon it
started over again,
this time with
Dwight and Evert.
Winona tugged at Jane's
sleeve. "Come with
me, please!" she said in Dakota.

Through the cornfields
they ran, to Winona's lodge.

Outside, Stands Sacred Woman and another
woman were rolling up a huge buffalo skin. They
greeted Jane.

"That is for our tioti, our winter house,"

Winona said. "Come inside, I want to show you my doll."

Winona's grandmother greeted them.

"Grandmother, I want Jane to see the doll you made me," Winona said.

"I only had a squash doll, but now Grandmother has made me this!"

She handed Jane the doll. It was beautiful. Dressed in deerskin, it was softly stuffed, and pleasant to cuddle. Her dress was fringed on the bottom, and tied with a sash in the middle. The sleeves and front of the dress were elaborately covered with tiny beads.

Lovingly, tenderly, Jane fingered the beads. She looked at Winona, whose face shone with the pleasure of sharing. Jane hugged the doll close to her. Her heart ached just a little. Winona reached over and patted Jane's knee.

Grandmother said something in Dakota so quickly that Jane did not understand.

"She asks if you have a doll," Winona said.

Jane shook her head.

Just then, a man came in the door.

"Grandfather!" Winona said. She ran to him and took him by the hand. "This is Jane."

Jane stood up. This, she knew, was Mahpiya

Wicasta, Chief Cloud Man.

He smiled at her. Jane liked his lined face.

Slowly, in Dakota, he asked her, "Little one, are you having fun today?"

Jane listened carefully, translating. When she

was certain she understood, she answered, "Yes."

"Good," he said, again smiling down at her. "A child is supposed to have fun."

Jane decided she liked Winona's grandfather. Samuel Pond spoke of Cloud Man as a great leader and a wise man, but Jane thought he was a very good grandfather, too.

Grandmother called Winona to her, handing her something. Winona came back to Jane with a cloth wrapped around a squash. It was rounded at the top, and long at the end, shaped a little like a baby. Wrapped as it was, it did look like a doll.

"Grandmother says you must have a squash baby," Winona said. "Bring your baby, I will bring mine, and we will play outside."

Happily holding her squash baby, Jane thanked Grandmother, said good-bye to Grandfather, and went out into the October sunshine.

Little Bird That Was Caught

Chapter Five

Samuel was chopping firewood outside his cabin. Jane was with him, squash doll in her arms.

"Did Red Cherry Woman give you that doll?" he asked.

"Canpadutawin?" Jane asked.

Smiling, Samuel said, "Yes. 'Red Cherry Woman' is English for Canpadutawin. W-I-N on the end of a name always means 'woman'. The Dakota have a very deep respect for women, for they are the life givers. They put the word 'woman' on the end of the name to show this great respect. They do not put 'man' on the end of men's names. It is good to see you are already thinking in Dakota, Jane. Can you read English?"

"Yes."

"Then come inside. I will show you how Gideon and I write down the Dakota words we learn using the English alphabet. Then you will be able to read in Dakota, too!"

Samuel bent down to gather up the wood he had chopped.

"Mr. Pond? Why do you say 'Dakota'? Most of the people at the fort say 'Sioux'."

Standing again now, his arms loaded with kindling, Samuel smiled down at her. His eyes were kind, Jane thought.

"'Dakota' is the name the people here call themselves. Other people gave them the name 'Sioux'. It is not a kind name, Jane, though many white people do not realize it."

"Why isn't it kind?"

"Because it was given to them by people who do not like them. In fact, the word 'Sioux' means 'enemy'."

"The Dakota people have enemies?"

"Every group of people has enemies. Long ago most peoples had enemies, and now, in places other than here, people make enemies of each other. It is no different now, I am afraid. It seems to be the way of the world."

He sighed, and in his quiet way, he seemed sad.

The fire crackled in the fireplace, and the Mission House was cozy with the warmth of company. The Pond brothers had been invited for supper, and now they all had gathered, telling stories of revivals, of travels, of home.

"Well, it will soon be time for more travels," Samuel said, stretching his long legs towards the fire.

Mrs. Stevens, knitting, looked up startled.

"What do you mean?" the reverend asked.

"I am going on the hunt. We leave in a day or two."

"What?" the reverend asked sharply.

"I am on a hunt of my own. A word hunt.

What better way to learn more Dakota language than to camp, stalk, kill game, and harvest with the Dakota people? I will learn many of their important words that way."

"But what about our work here?" the reverend asked. "Isn't that more important? Dakota words! What about the Word of God?"

"Many of the Dakota people have learned some English, sir," Samuel said. "But the only way we can successfully spread the word of God to them is by learning their language."

"Most of the Dakota will be gone for the hunt," Gideon added. "And I will be here."

The reverend sat back in his chair, crossing his arms across his chest. He fell into a gloomy silence. Then he sat forward again. "I want you two brothers to consider moving in here. I cannot possibly make any headway in my work with you so far away. The center of the mission must be right here. We have room, your place is small."

Gideon and Samuel exchanged uncomfortable looks.

"Well, Mr. Stevens, our cabin is only a mile away. We have a garden there, and our cow. We built the cabin, and have lived there for a year," Gideon said. "You were aware, sir, of where our cabin was when you chose this site. My brother and I are not anxious to move, and I am sure we can continue our work without interfering with yours."

"Interfering? You work for me!" the reverend said.

Again the brothers looked at each other.

"We will consider your offer, sir," Samuel said.

Lucy stood up, saying, "Let us sing! Do you sing, Mr. Samuel Pond?"

Samuel gave a resounding laugh. "No, ma'am! I greatly enjoy hearing others sing, but my own talents are sadly lacking in that area!"

So Lucy began a song, and Mrs. Stevens sang harmony. Gideon and the reverend added their voices, and even Dwight and Evert shyly joined in. Jane did not know the words.

She felt hollow inside. Suddenly, Samuel Pond held out his arms, and she climbed onto his lap. Tears began slipping down her cheeks.

When the singing stopped, no one said anything about Jane's tears, but Samuel held her for a long time.

The next evening, those in the Mission House heard a loud voice coming from the village.

They stopped to listen.

It was a man's voice, speaking in Dakota. Jane thought perhaps it was Chief Cloud Man. He spoke for a long time, as if this were a speech. Briefly, others spoke, and then there was silence.

Jane and Evert rushed to the window, but could see only a few fires outside of the lodges, their merry flickering decorating the darkness.

"Come away from the window, children!" Mrs. Stevens said sharply. "And go to bed."

There was nothing to do but watch. Jane stood on the prairie, watching her friends go away. The Dakota children were excited as they ran around, helping the adults. Jane waved to Chaske and Harpen.

Gideon had told her that the voice in the night had indeed been Chief Cloud Man's. After talking with the others in the village about this year's hunt, he had made decisions based on their wishes. His speech had been information and directions for the morning when they would leave for the hunt.

Their few horses were being loaded for the trip, and so were the dogs. There were no wagons. Instead, the horses and dogs were fitted with long poles on both sides, with a harness holding them on. On these poles was a frame where clothing, bedding, and cooking pots were securely tied. Jane saw that a cradleboard had been hung on one, and the baby We-harka was being snugly nestled into it. Her mother and grandmother both carried packs on their backs, as did most of the other women, older men, and the stronger children. The hunters carried guns and traps.

Waa-bec scurried past on an errand for his father, Badger. He grinned at Jane, calling, "In the spring, more turtle soup!"

The sounds of leaving, of dogs barking, babies crying, adults giving directions, filled the air. Then, little by little, they started off. Stands Sacred Woman was hard at work, beautifully elegant even now. Jane felt a lump in her throat.

Winona, clad in a warm blanket and leather leggings, came running up. "Grandfather says we will be back here for our winter camp," she said, smiling her lovely smile at Jane. "Maybe you can come to my tioti this winter, and hear stories!"

With that she hurried to catch up with Stands Sacred Woman and the rest of her family.

At the Pond cabin, Samuel had finished packing for the hunting trip. Gideon was also packing to move in with the Stevenses.

"I am not sure this is wise, Samuel," Gideon said. "And I would much prefer to live here, but for the sake of the mission, I will try to live over there."

Samuel looked around a bit sadly at the cabin. "I am not sure it is wise either. I will be back in the winter, and we can talk then."

Jane waited quietly. She had been sent to help Gideon. Samuel turned to her, and took her chin tenderly into his hand, saying, "Good-bye, Miss Jane. I will think of you while I am gone. Always remember, you are greatly loved by our Heavenly Father."

And then he was gone, too.

She awoke one morning to gray skies. All the golden color of autumn was gone now. By afternoon, a light snow had begun to fall.

The reverend was at the fort, preaching. He had offered to bring Mrs. Clark back with him. Jane was delighted.

Mrs. Stevens had not come out of her room that day, and Jane wondered if she was sick. Cousin Lucy made meals, but she did not seem her cheerful self. Instead, she walked often to the window and peered out.

"Oh, please, dear Lord, do not let it snow

yet!" Lucy prayed aloud.

As daylight ebbed and the snow thickened, they heard the sounds of horses, and soon the reverend came in with Mrs. Clark.

Jane expected a happy reunion, but Lucy met them at the door saying urgently, "You are needed upstairs right away! I am so glad you have come!"

Mrs. Clark disappeared with Lucy without so much as a hello to Jane. The reverend was quiet as usual, but now he paced back and forth, filling the woodbox himself, instead of telling the boys to do so. He did not leave the house, and even seemed to be having difficulty reading.

Jane played with her squash doll, staying out of his way.

When it had been dark for a long time and Jane was wondering if anyone would feed her before she had to go to sleep, she heard a sound from

upstairs, like that of a baby crying.

Reverend Stevens, sitting by the fire, bowed his head and began praying. Jane thought she could see tears on his cheeks.

The baby was little and red, and her name was Lucy Anne. Everyone seemed glad she was here, even though she did not do anything but sleep.

It snowed and snowed. Lucy began teaching Jane, Evert, and Dwight at the big table each day. Mrs. Stevens cared for the baby, and sometimes seemed to forget that Jane was there. The reverend was restless, and when weather permitted, traveled to the fort to preach.

Gideon Pond now lived with them. He built a cradle for Lucy Anne, but mostly he worked on a book of the Dakota language. Each day he brought in milk from the cow he and Samuel owned, and smiled as the children drank it.

The days were long and cold, the nights even longer and colder. Often, Jane went to the window and looked out at the wintery world. The summer houses in the Dakota village stood silent, dark, and forlorn. But one day she heard a sound that drew her to the window. She heard hoof beats.

Samuel was back!

In the evenings, they listened to his stories of the hunt.

"It is hard, demanding work for everyone," Samuel said. "For the hunters, it means hours and hours each day, wading through deep snows, braving fierce winds, sometimes without sighting any deer. Often they come back with smaller game such as raccoons, occasionally a bear or elk, but sometimes with nothing at all. Of course, they are good hunters, and when a hunter returns to camp with a carcass, the children have a wonderful way of announcing his return.

"The hunters go out in small groups, and when one man kills a deer, he gives a special shout, one used only for this. If no one comes, the deer is all his. If one man comes, they share it. The first three to arrive have a right to share it."

"Why in the world would they share their kill when it is so difficult?" asked Mrs. Stevens, patting Lucy Anne on the back.

"It encourages less skillful hunters. They do not have to return to their families empty-handed, and everyone still needs to be fed despite who has obtained it. The successful hunter is saved from carrying it back by himself, and he always keeps the hide."

"A kind and generous plan," Lucy mused.

"But what about the children?" Jane ventured to ask.

Samuel smiled at her. "When a hunter returns, the children see that he has a deer. They call, 'Oo-koo-hoo! Oo-koo-hoo!' so loudly all in camp can hear. As soon as they see who the hunter is, they announce his name, just as loudly. By nightfall, everyone in camp knows who is back, and what he has caught."

"Winona and Waa-bec call out, too?" she asked.

"Yes, Waa-bec is amongst the loudest!" Samuel said heartily. "And, Miss Jane, you will be glad to know both of those friends should be back here soon. I think the children enjoy the hunt, but it is much work and discomfort, and often I heard children crying in the cold until the new camp was set up. It is not an easy life, and is hardest on the youngest."

"I had never wanted to mention this before, but I have noticed how dirty some of the Sioux people seem," Lucy said, looking cautiously at Samuel.

"Well, if we lived in tents most of the year with no conveniences for washing, and very few items of clothing, we would find it difficult to keep a clean appearance, too," he said. "But the question, if there is any, is not whether or not they are clean, but whether or not they are as clean as they can be under the circumstances. I found cleanliness very difficult for myself while on the hunt."

He laughed, and Gideon joined him.

"Please tell us," Lucy urged.

"I wanted to wash in the tent in which I was a guest, but when I asked for a bowl to wash up in, I was told none could be spared, for if I washed in it, the bowl could never again be used for food. Does that help you see what high standards they have within their homes?"

Lucy nodded. "Certainly, but what is so amusing, Mr. Pond?"

"I decided to use the snow to wash up, and most of the Dakota smiled and shook their heads at me, as I stood shivering in the cold, rubbing my face and arms with snow. It was a miserable experience, and I think they thought I was rather unwise, but they were kind," Samuel said, chuckling again at himself. "However, about once a month, the women cut holes in the ice and go into the lake, in their clothes up to their waists, to bathe and wash their clothing. They build fires on the shore to dry off."

Jane shivered.

"It is not fair, perhaps," said Lucy, "for one who has a warm bath to make comparisons."

Jane moved closer to the fire.

Just outside the cluster of bark lodges, the cone-shaped tipi began to appear, for many of the hunting party had returned. Jane watched with delight as the poles went up, and the skins were stretched expertly over them. Winona, Waa-bec,

Haparm, and Harpen were back!

It was not long before Winona, her winter moccasins making soft prints in the snow, came to the Mission House door. She asked eagerly to see the baby. Mrs. Stevens proudly showed her Lucy Anne who looked back at Winona with interest.

Then Winona said to Jane, "My grandmother asks that you come to see her, Jane."

Jane translated for Mrs. Stevens.

"Why would her grandmother want to see you?" Mrs. Stevens said doubtfully.

Evert, looking up from his studies, said quietly, "I think, Mother, that Winona is indeed asking Jane to see her grandmother."

Nodding at Jane, Mrs. Stevens leaned over to put Lucy Anne into her cradle. Grabbing her coat, Jane ran off with Winona.

The air was so cold her cheeks and forehead soon ached. A tioti was being put up and Jane marveled at the four women working in the cold. Three long poles had been tied together below their tops. Nine smaller poles were being placed with their tops in the upper forks of the longer poles, and spread out to form the base of the tioti. A covering of buffalo skins would be securely attached to them.

Now she stepped inside Stands Sacred

Woman's tioti. Jane knew it belonged to Winona's mother, as did the summer lodge, for all homes belonged to the Dakota women.

It was dark inside, except for the cheery fire. The outside was made of eight buffalo skins, sewn carefully together with sinews. These were lined with another layer to trap cold air. The lining was covered with drawings. Jane was surprised how warm it was, but her eyes smarted from the smoke. She noticed the pile of cozy buffalo robes and feather pillows for beds. Each bed lay on an animal skin, which kept the rain and night dampness from seeping in. Behind them were large rawhide sacks that Jane thought looked like envelopes. These served as cupboards for extra clothing or meat. The family's dishes were neatly stacked near the fire.

Winona's grandmother, Red Cherry Woman, was sitting on one bed, working on some small moccasins. She greeted Jane and patted the robe beside her. Jane and Winona settled down on either side of her. Winona sat with her legs curled under her to the right, as Grandmother did.

"I thought of you many times while we were gone, little Jane," Red Cherry Woman said in Dakota. "So I made something for you."

She placed a doll into Jane's arms, a beautiful,

soft doll of deer skin, decorated with dozens of tiny beads. Two blue beads had been sewn on for the doll's eyes, and a small red bead formed her mouth.

"Oh!" Jane uttered, hugging the doll to her chest. "Oh, Grandmother! Thank you! I will name her for you— 'Red Cherry Woman'!" Winona's grandmother laughed a laugh of tenderness.

One day Waa-bec asked Jane to come into his tioti. He had made some tops that he wanted to lend to Evert. Inside, she saw several men seated around the fire, deep in conversation. It was very crowded, and knowing it was not respectful to walk in front of people as they spoke, Jane waited by the door for Waa-bec.

He made his way over to her, handed her the tops and said quietly, "It is good that you did not step over the men's feet."

Outside, she saw Gideon Pond walking

through the village, his long legs making great strides.

"Mr. Pond, I have a question," Jane said boldly.

"There is 'a time to keep silence, and a time to speak,' Ecclesiastes 3:6. This is a time to speak," Gideon answered, smiling down at her. "Ask away, Miss Jane!"

"When I was in Waa-bec's tioti, there were men visiting with his father. Waa-bec said it was good I did not step over their feet. Do you know why?"

Gideon laughed a little. "Yes, I do know, Jane. The men believe that if a woman steps over their feet, they will never be able to run fast."

Puzzled, Jane looked up at him.

"It does not seem likely, does it?" he said. "But then, all groups of people have beliefs that do not make sense to others. Before we judge, we should ask where that belief came from. Sometimes you find out that long, long ago, there was good reason for something that no longer has any reason, just superstition."

"Lucy says superstition is evil," Jane said.

"I suppose it can be if it leads to someone being hurt. This one does not seem to be harmful. But I find that in life, some things are very bad and some things are very good, but most things are in between. We must watch and decide before we quickly say something is good or bad."

Jane nodded. Gideon, she thought, would make a good papa.

"Now, Miss Jane, would you like to hear all of the Dakota words I learned and wrote down today?"

They walked on towards the Mission House, reciting words into the winter twilight.

Classes started in the new schoolhouse now that most of the Dakota children were back. Every morning, Lucy marched Dwight, Evert, and Jane over there, always looking towards the village, hoping that some of the children there would join them. But these coldest months of winter gave Dakota families a time of quiet, the only time all year they could rest. No one seemed to notice the small parade to the schoolhouse.

Samuel often stopped by, quizzing the children and Lucy on Dakota words and pronunciations. Once in a while, he even asked Jane if she knew how to pronounce certain words, for he wanted to speak the language perfectly himself.

It snowed some days, and when the sun did

come out, it brought a bitter cold with it. Still, the schoolhouse seemed warm when Samuel was there.

"Oh, dear! Aunt Julia? I think you had better come see this," Lucy said one morning as she was about to comb Jane's long hair.

Mrs. Stevens came to look. "Oh, Jane, you are covered with lice!"

The two women looked at each other in disgust, and Jane shivered at the thought.

"Well, there is nothing to be done but to cut off your hair," Mrs. Stevens said. "Lucy, get the scissors."

"No! Please, no!" Jane protested, but she was ignored. Soon piles of blonde hair were tossed outside, and Jane was thoroughly shampooed.

Dwight came in, and pointed at Jane's shorn head. He began laughing loudly.

"Do not laugh so soon, Dwight Stevens," his mother said sternly. "Lice are catching, you know. You may be next."

That day, Jane learned two more Dakota words. Finding herself surrounded by the other children, she interpreted their words: shaved and head. Shaved Head. No longer was she called Jane. She was Shaved Head.

Waa-Bec took special delight in teasing her, running his hand quickly over her head and taunting, "Shaved Head!" Then he would grin, laughing heartily.

Jane laughed back, for she knew from watching the others that a person who was playfully teased was a person who was greatly liked.

There was another change, in addition to her name. Slowly the Dakota children began coming to school. When they came to the Mission House door each day to ask Jane to play, Lucy urged her to get them to come to school instead. More books had arrived, and Lucy was anxious to attract students. "Ask them to come to the schoolhouse with you," she suggested.

Winona, Harpen, and her sister, Harpstenah, did come with Jane, staying as close to her as possible. Jane whispered words of encouragement. She even hinted that there might be a reward. And indeed there was, for Lucy had a supply of turnips, and each little girl received some for coming to school. As the days went by, three more children came out of curiosity, but also because they knew Lucy or Shaved Head would give them turnips after classes were over.

They sang, for Lucy knew that a good way to teach English and Bible stories was through song. Some days, Lucy gave away a whole bushel of turnips. She was happy, for teaching was the reason she had come all this long way. And Jane, Dwight, and Evert were glad, for class was much more interesting when the Dakota children came.

Jane had rounded the corner with an armload of firewood when she saw the reverend go into the house.

"Julia," Jane heard him call, irritation grating his voice. "I just saw Dwight and Evert running with the Sioux boys. I do not want our children associating with the Indian children."

Mrs. Stevens answered nervously, "Oh, Jedediah, do you know what you are asking?"

"I am not asking. I am telling you."

"Jedediah, please listen. We have brought our children to this wilderness. We can provide them with no other playmates but the Indian children."

"They are heathens. Your children are playing with heathens, Julia!"

Mrs. Stevens persisted gently. "But they are also children. Perhaps our children will be a good influence."

"Well, I do not mind so much with the girl, but I do not like my sons associating with heathens' children!"

"Often, Dwight and Evert are too busy with chores and studies to play," Mrs. Stevens said.

"All right. But only sometimes. Watch them carefully, Julia, lest they lose sight of God."

Quietly, Jane set the wood down outside of the door and ran off to find Dwight and Evert. She would warn them to play farther from the house from now on.

It was so cold, the children could not play outside. After her studies and chores were finished, Jane was allowed to find the other girls. Today they played in Winona's tioti. Harpen, Harpstenah, and Waska were there, too, all with dolls. Grandmother and Stands Sacred Woman were sewing and enjoying the girls' play.

Harpen was pretending to be the mother. Suddenly, Winona stopped and turned to Jane.

"Shaved Head, what do white children call their mothers?"

"Mama, Ma, or Mother," said Jane.

"Why don't you call Mrs. Stevens that?"

"She is not my mother."

Jane was aware that Winona's mother and grandmother exchanged glances.

"Where is your mother?" asked Waska.

"In New York," Jane said.

She looked around the tioti, at the faces of her friends, at the woman she called "Grandmother," and at Winona's loving mother. And she began to tell them. Slowly, in halting Dakota, she told them of her mother's injury, her papa, her brothers and sisters, Mrs. Vedder, and the year-long journey with the Stevens family. She talked for a long, long time, until she was tired of thinking in Dakota. But she had told it all.

From that moment, everything was different. Her Dakota friends had always been kind, but now they were as a family to her. Her story traveled from tioti to tioti, and everyone felt for the child who had been taken from her family.

No longer was she called "Shaved Head."

She was Zitkadan Usawin. "Little Bird That Was Caught."

In February the weather warmed for a few days so the reverend went to Fort Snelling for supplies. Mrs. Stevens and Lucy did a large washing of clothes.

"Go and see what the other children are
doing on this beautiful day," Mrs. Stevens said.

They did not need to be told twice. Dwight,
Evert, and Jane raced to the lake's edge, where Waa-
bec, Harpen, Chaske, Haparm, and Winona were
gathered.

"We're playing the Sticking-Together Game,"
Waa-bec said. "Everyone has a top, and we whip
them on the ice to get them to bump together.
Whichever one out-bumps and out-spins the other,
wins."

They all crouched down to watch the little
tops whirl on the ice. The warm, damp wind
whipped through Jane's hair, which again had grown
down around her ears. She shouted along with the
others, clapping as Winona's top out-spun the others.

Chief Cloud Man stopped, smiling at the
children before going about his business.

Then Chaske said, "Let's sled!"

The Dakota boys ran off, each returning with
something that the new children could not identify.

"Are they bones?" Evert asked in Dakota.

"Buffalo ribs," Waa-bec said, patting his own
ribs.

"Those are the sleds!" Dwight said in
English.

"Come on!" Waa-bec urged.

And down the hill they slid, taking turns on the ribs, screaming and shouting and laughing until the sun set.

The Dakota children came often to school now. Lucy spoke Dakota quite well, and with a basket of turnips at her side, she taught Bible stories, English words, and arithmetic. Now Samuel taught the older children, but he always walked home with Jane.

One day, slowing his long stride for Jane to keep up, he said, "Well, Miss Jane, I hear you are now called 'Zitkadan Usawin'."

She nodded.

"And I heard why. That is quite a story you have, quite a life you have lived already!" He smiled down at her. "I want you to know that even though you are very far away from your family, you do have family here. The Dakota people love you, and so do Gideon and I."

It was bitterly cold, but Jane felt warm all over.

They opened the door to angry voices. Gideon and Reverend Stevens were arguing with a strength that sent fear flooding through Jane.

"My brother and I have been working on this since before you even arrived! You cannot claim any credit for it!" Gideon fumed.

"You work for me. So anything that comes from this mission must come through me," the reverend answered, his voice quavering.

"How can you claim credit for Samuel's book? It is a spelling book of Dakota words. You do not even speak the language! How could you have written it? How can you dare think of putting your name on the title page?"

Samuel was pulling off his coat, listening. When he heard this, the coat dropped to the floor as he hurried off to join the argument.

Jane picked up his coat and hung it on a peg by the door. Then she hung up her own quietly, knowing something terrible would come of this.

She was right.

Spring was coming, a time of hope, but at the Lake Harriet Mission, there was little feeling of hope in the air. Most of the Dakota people had left again, this time for the sugar camp, where they would make maple sugar. School was held in the Mission House for Dwight, Jane, and Evert. The sky was bleak, the ground still covered with old snow, except where patches of mud showed through. But worst of all, Gideon had left and Samuel was strangely silent.

There had been more arguments before Gideon left. The reverend wanted him to chop wood for the fires, tend the cow, and do other chores. Gideon and Samuel pointed out that they were there for the same reasons as the reverend: to tell the Dakota people about Jesus. They were working on their language skills to do this. The reverend argued that they must take orders from him, for he was the only one who was an ordained minister. Therefore, he was in charge and they must do the type of work he chose. Besides, because they were not ordained, the reverend felt, the Pond brothers were not proper-ly trained to teach the faith to the Dakota.

One day the brothers returned from a trip to the fort. Gideon announced he was leaving for Lac qui Parle, the mission run by the Williamsons and Sarah. Now there was an emptiness where Gideon had been. Jane missed his quick smile, his questions for the Dakota people about every word they used, his way of telling Jane of God's love, not God's wrath.

Jane clung to the back of the reverend as the horse pranced over the prairie. Gideon's leaving had made him more determined to reach the Dakota people, for he had had little success so far. Some of the villagers were off spearing muskrats, but many were at their sugar camp, and the reverend had decided to go there to preach. He needed an inter-preter so he took Jane. There was only one horse, and as she was the smallest of the children who spoke both languages, it was easiest to take her.

Soon they saw the weathered skins of the tipi, and smelled smoke in the air. The camp was set in a grove of maple, birch, and box elder trees.

Their arrival was announced by cries from the children, who came running alongside them as they had so many months ago. Both were greeted, Jane warmly, the reverend politely.

All around them, people were busy tapping trees and collecting sap. Jane saw little birch bark troughs in the trunks of the maple trees. A great fire burned where the sap was being carefully boiled down. The snow was wet in the March sun, and Jane noticed how soaked most of the Dakotas' moccasins were. Everyone was cheerful, but Jane, clad in Evert's warm, old boots, wondered how they could be.

The reverend began to preach, with Jane at his side calling out his words in Dakota. As she struggled to change the English words into Dakota, she was aware that the reverend was trying very hard to be patient with her.

But no one seemed to notice. They all went on with their work.

Too soon, Jane was back on the horse, riding in the damp wind at twilight. The reverend was disgusted, and told Jane so.

"They did not even listen to me!"

Jane hardly ever spoke to the reverend, but now there was something she must explain. She remembered seeing Chief Cloud Man standing outside the lodges to give a speech. No one had been outside to hear it, but they were listening in their homes. "Reverend Stevens," she said, "the Dakota people do not listen in the same way we do. They listen with their ears, but do not need to look at the speaker."

"What do you mean?"

"I heard Waa-bec's father say once that white men must listen with their eyes, for they always look at the speaker."

"So you are saying that maybe they did hear me today?"

"Perhaps," Jane said.

She felt very grown up.

The sun grew stronger each day. Some families returned from the sugar camp.

Jane stood back from the game before her, watching Evert and Dwight, on opposite teams, line up with Waa-bec, Chaske, Haparm and others. This was the Throwing-at-Each-Other-with-Mud Game, and Jane saw the boys were armed with a collection of mud balls. They advanced upon each other, mud balls wobbling on the end of springy sticks.

Zing! Waa-bec flung the first mud ball. Splat! It hit Dwight on the chest. Jane could tell it hurt, but he flung one back, now ducking to avoid another shot. Back and forth the two teams flung the balls, laughing and yelling, until these were gone and the boys were covered with mud.

Spring was here!

Jane sat by the lake edge, holding her doll close to her chest. The cold from the ground was seeping through her petticoats and dress, but she did not care, for Jane wanted to be all alone to cry.

Today Samuel had left.

Jane had known Samuel was unhappy. He was as angry with the reverend as Gideon, and Jane knew when Gideon announced he was leaving that Samuel might have plans to leave, too. When Samuel remained silent, Jane hoped he would stay. But, of course, he was only waiting for a letter to make his plans.

He was traveling all the way to Connecticut, to become a minister. Then, if he came back, Reverend Stevens could not tell him what to do.

He had seemed sad to leave. He told Jane he

would think of her often, and pray for her. She would think of him often. She silently said a prayer for him now.

A few geese flew over the water, for they were returning after the long winter. But Samuel was gone, and Jane did not know if he would ever come back.

She buried her face in her doll and cried.

A Dutiful Grandchild

Chapter Six

It was lonesome with the Pond brothers gone. Whenever she could, Jane played with the Dakota children, or joined Winona's family in their tioti. She stirred the pot of beans and buffalo fat that Stands Sacred Woman was cooking. Grandmother showed Jane how to fashion a moccasin and roast corn.

One day as Jane left the house, Mrs. Stevens called after her, "Jane! Come back in an hour. I want you to take care of Lucy Anne."

Jane found much excitement in the village, for the others who had not returned in winter had now come back, laden with furs. It soon would be time to take down the tipi and move to the summer bark lodges. Jane enjoyed herself, greeting those who had just arrived and hearing them marvel at how much Dakota she could now speak. She forgot all about taking care of Lucy Anne.

She was helping Red Cherry Woman and Stands Sacred Woman pack up their bowls and kettles when Mrs. Stevens suddenly appeared at the door. Everyone was startled, for Mrs. Stevens had never once come to the homes of the Dakota people.

Jane saw that she was angry, and she carried a switch, the kind she had seen the reverend use to thrash Dwight and Evert. Quickly, Jane hid behind Stands Sacred Woman.

"Jane," Mrs. Stevens said, her voice quavering. "Come home."

Jane stood still, but Stands Sacred Woman moved slightly, to shield Jane even more.

Peeking out, Jane saw that now Lucy stood with Mrs. Stevens.

"Jane," Mrs. Stevens commanded. "You have disobeyed me and you will be punished."

"She will not come," Stands Sacred Woman said firmly in Dakota, "until you have thrown away that stick. We will not let her leave here unless we can be assured that you will not hit her."

Mrs. Stevens looked confused, for she did not understand what was being said to her. Lucy whispered a translation, and then said slowly in Dakota, "My aunt wants you to know that Jane is not your child, and this is not her home. She is to come back to her home, and what happens there is our business."

Now Red Cherry Woman stepped forward. She said, "Little Bird is not really your child. She is just as much our child as she is yours. The Mission House is not her home. She prefers to be here."

Lucy, looking pale, translated for Mrs. Stevens, whose eyes widened as she understood.

Red Cherry Woman spoke again. "You are welcome to visit us. But we will protect Little Bird. If she is hurt, we will know. We must care for her, for the sake of her mother who does not know where she is."

Again Lucy translated, and she and Mrs. Stevens, looking uneasy, left the doorway. They had a hasty, whispered conversation. Then Mrs. Stevens threw the stick down, and they left.

Red Cherry Woman picked up the stick and threw it on the fire. She watched Mrs. Stevens and Lucy retreat. Jane stayed at the tioti the rest of the day. When she returned to the Mission House, Stands Sacred Woman and two other women accompanied her. They stood in the doorway, looking calmly but firmly at Mrs. Stevens.

"I will not hit her," Mrs. Stevens said quietly. Then they left.

Mrs. Stevens did not speak to Jane that evening, but she did not punish her in any way.

"Look!" Winona said, her eyes shining. She and Jane crouched down to peer at the green plants at their feet. "Strawberries! I must tell Grandmother so she can soak the seed corn."

Jane wondered what strawberries had to do with corn.

"When the strawberry plants are out, it is warm enough for corn to be planted! Come, let's go tell Grandmother, so she can soak the seeds. When they have sprouted, we will help her plant."

As they headed back to the village, something caught Jane's eye.

"What is that?" she asked, seeing some cloth on a large stone.

Winona paused. "It is an offering. Someone was praying here. They left the cloth. Sometimes they leave tobacco, or a hatchet."

The cloth lay in the warm sun, and Jane was conscious of the quiet around them. She remembered hearing Samuel telling Reverend Stevens that he did not think the Dakota people believed in one god but rather many gods or spirits.

"Winona, do you pray?" Jane asked.

"Yes, of course," Winona said. "I say a thank you to the spirits of the animals that gave their lives for my food. Or sometimes, when I hear a ghost whistle at night, I pray it won't come and hurt me."

"You think there are ghosts?" Jane asked.

"Oh, yes. And the bird that is the voice of thunder, that is an important spirit. But many people also speak of Unkteri. It is the spirit of a great animal, bigger than the buffalo! My uncle has some of its bones. They are very holy. Do you pray, Little Bird?"

Jane nodded. "I have to pray with the Stevenses. I liked praying with the Pond brothers. Sometimes at night, when I am alone, I pray, too."

Winona nodded. "There are spirits all around," she said. "Wherever you are and whatever you are doing, it is important to speak to them."

They were beyond the little altar now, but neither of the friends left behind the questions it had brought.

The gentle May sun warmed Jane's shoulders

as she joined Winona, Stands Sacred Woman, and Red Cherry Woman in their garden.

Gardening had always been women's work, Red Cherry Woman explained to Jane, and men always did the hunting. Other foods, like wild rice, plums, and water lilies, were gathered from the wild. In this way, the Dakota families could have enough food, if all worked together. Winona must learn the jobs women do, and Jane was welcome to learn, too.

"Your grandfather, Cloud Man, thinks the day will come when we cannot get enough food in this way. Many disagree with him, but he wants to try some of the white people's ways of planting. The people who have come to this village with him agreed to try the new ways, but still the men are not certain that they should work the crops. They are learning to use the plow Grizzly Bear brought, and so now the fields are ready to plant. Women always did all the digging of a field with digging sticks and hoes. Still, we women want to do the planting and harvesting," she explained.

Jane knew she meant Samuel when she said Grizzly Bear.

"Mrs. Stevens and Lucy are deciding where to plant their garden," Jane said.

"Well, Little Bird, tell them Red Cherry

Woman says to look for the wild artichoke. That is where the soil is best."

Now they knelt in the moist soil. Jane and Winona dug holes with their hands and dropped in the sprouted seeds.

"This corn will not grow as tall as the corn Grizzly Bear plants, but it can be harvested earlier," Stands Sacred Woman explained. "When the seeds have three or four leaves, we will loosen the soil around them with our hands. You can help, too. Then we will make hills around each plant, using our hoes."

"Do you plant squash, too?" Jane asked, thinking of her squash baby.

"Yes, in a few days," Red Cherry Woman said. "And beans. We have already planted the sun-flowers," she said, pointing towards another field."

"Soon we will need the stages to keep the blackbirds out of the corn," Stands Sacred Woman said, patting the loose soil over some seeds. "Little Bird, you can help Winona and me keep the birds away this year."

"You learn fast, Little Bird. Work over there now," Red Cherry Woman said, handing her more seeds.

Like a dutiful grandchild, Jane knelt down,

feeling the moistness on her knees and the sun on her back.

"Jane, you are a great big girl of seven now," Mrs. Stevens said one June day. "You are old enough to take care of Lucy Anne while you play with the other girls. Keep her in the shade."

Tucking a blanket into a large willow basket, she placed Lucy Anne in it. The baby was seven months old, rosy and round. She sported two teeth and could sit up, but she had not yet begun to crawl.

Outside, Jane's friends were calling to her, "Zitkadan Usawin!"

Taking turns carrying the basket and baby, Jane and her friends headed to the village. The tipi were packed away and in this season, life revolved around the bark lodges that were large and close together. Each one was made of a frame of wooden poles that were tied together with basswood bark. Sheets of ash or elm bark covered the poles, forming the walls. A deer hide served as a door, and there was a smoke hole in the roof for an inside fire.

Most houses had a scaffold in front where corn was dried, or furs hung. Scaffolds were also happy places for sitting in the shade to talk and play games. Today they went to Harpen's lodge, where her mother and friends were playing the Shooting-Dice-with-a-Basket Game under their scaffold. They had three pairs of dice, all made of plum stones. Harpen's mother, Bird Feather Woman, showed them to Jane. One pair had a tiny painting of a buffalo, the second had a bird called a swallow, and the last was painted all black. After Jane admired them, Bird Feather Woman placed them into a small basket, shook it, and turned the dice out. There was a cheer, for the pair of buffalo dice turned face up, and the swallow dice face down. Ten points! There was much score keeping, and the game went on for a long time.

Lucy Anne enjoyed being petted and fussed over by the Dakota women, but now she was tired. Just as she started to cry, a loud shout went up, and all turned to see a group of men running after a rolling hoop. They were trying to throw five-foot-long spears through the inside of the hoop. Jane and Lucy Anne watched the shouting and laughing men who were sometimes successful.

Jane knew that much betting went on with many of the games, and the reverend did not approve. Samuel had said that the villagers worked hard, but they also knew how to play. Jane did not understand any of this, but she knew that the

Dakota people knew more games than anyone else!

Jane stepped inside Waska's bark lodge. It was roomy and airy, unlike the Mission House, which was hot and stuffy these days. Around three walls were frames covered with skins. These were the beds, chairs or couches, all the furniture the Dakota people had.

Waska's mother, Good Star Woman, had just finished feeding her baby. Now she placed him into the cradleboard his father's sisters had made. She wrapped her tiny son in a woolen cloth she had embroidered before he was born. She folded a smaller cloth into a pillow of sorts, and put that on the cradleboard, placing the baby on the board, his head on this tiny pillow. The cradleboard had wooden sides, and because of the blanket the baby was tucked between the sides very securely. A strip of bark formed a circular guard over his head, and more strips came down from this to protect his body. Attached to this guard was a light cloth that hung down in front of the baby, keeping wind, sun, and insects away from his face. He was safe, securely wrapped, no matter how much movement his mother made. "Now he is comfortable," said Good Star Woman, caressing his cheek gently.

Finally, his mother tied a small pouch onto the cradleboard. It was in the shape of a lizard, and covered with beads.

"That is pretty," Jane said in her best Dakota. "All babies have these—turtles for girls,

snakes or lizards for boys," Good Star Woman
explained. "After a baby is born, he still has a small
piece of the umbilical cord on his belly. When that
heals and drops off, we place it in this special pouch.
We keep it with the baby to protect him, hoping he
will have a long life."

Turning to Waska she said, "My daughter,
would you get more sphagnum moss?"

Jane knew what it was for. Dakota babies did
not have cloth diapers like Lucy Anne. Instead,
mothers and grandmothers gently packed this soft
moss or silky cattail down around a baby's bottom,
and placed a cloth tied with leather around it. When
the moss or down was wet, they quickly replaced it.

Outside the Mission House, white diapers
flapped in the summer breeze. There certainly were
many ways of taking care of a baby.

Summer was busy for Jane. When she finished her chores at the Mission House, she took
Lucy Anne and played with the Dakota girls. Their
favorite quiet game was Cat's Cradle, where they
twisted strings into many shapes.

Often, however, she worked with Winona as
Red Cherry Woman and Stands Sacred Woman
taught them many skills. Grandmother guided Jane's

hands as she struggled to weave a mat out of cattails, or grappled with the ribbons she was using to embroider a shirt.

One day Grandmother gave her a scrap of deer hide. For hours, Jane labored to make a tiny, shapeless doll. She added a few beads. Jane told Grandmother she was going to give it to Lucy Anne when she was old enough.

Grandmother turned the doll over in her workworn hands, touching the beadwork. She smiled and nodded. Jane knew she had done a good job, and that she was a generous grandchild.

The corn, beans, squash, potatoes, and pumpkins needed hoeing during the summer months, and she and Winona laughed and chatted as they worked. Winona was quick to spot foods that Jane would pass by, so she guided Jane as they followed the women. There were blueberries and nuts and turnips. Stands Sacred Woman seemed to know of everything that was edible in the wild, and how to find it. She made certain Winona and Jane learned, too.

Jane was collecting firewood for the baking of the Mission House bread when she noticed several women in the lake. They were standing in water up to their chests, and each seemed to be moving something under the water with her feet. Jane stopped to watch.

"Zitkadan Usawin!"

Jane turned to see Waa-bec coming towards her.

"Waa-bec, what are they doing?" Jane asked, pointing to the women in the water.

"They are collecting psincha, a kind of food. It is about this big," he said, forming his fingers to make a round inch. "It grows underwater, so they must find it by feeling. They pull it up with their feet. It does not float, so they must hold onto it with their toes, raising their legs high enough until they can reach it with their hands."

Jane watched for a while longer.

"Ask if you can swim," Waa-bec urged.

"I cannot ask until I have gathered firewood," Jane said.

"Come then, I'll help you," Waa-bec said.

Clad in clothes that they had outgrown, Jane,

Dwight, and Evert sat astride logs, paddling around Lake Harriet with Waa-Bec, Winona, Chaske, Haparm, Harpen, and Waska. The logs were their horses, and they shrieked with silliness as they splashed and bumped each other off.

Struggling to stay afloat once she was in the water, Jane wiped the water from her eyes. She noticed that the Dakota boys swam differently from the Dakota girls, and both swam differently than Dwight and Evert. The boys made a rolling motion as they turned first from one side, then to the other. The girls held their feet closely together, striking the water with the top of their feet to move forward. It reminded Jane a little of the steamboat wheels.

"You boys do not swim like the girls do," Jane said when Waa-bec swam closer to her.

"Of course we don't. Boys and girls wouldn't swim the same way, silly!" he said.

After hours of play, they gathered on the shore and feasted again on turtle soup and clams. The wind was July-warm, drying their hair and clothing quickly.

As the reverend was at the fort, Dwight and Evert could go to the village with Jane and the other children. There they stopped to watch a game of

Using Bones. It was the only game Jane had seen men and women play together.

Teams of men and women held deer leg bones. In each leg, four holes had been made, and loops of beads were attached. Six of these legs were strung onto a deerskin string, which was knotted on one end. A wooden pin was on the other end. Each player must swing the bones up upon the pin.

The other children stayed to watch, but Winona wanted Jane to come home with her. Outside of her lodge, Stands Sacred Woman was working on a buffalo hide stretched out on a frame that she had made. Scraping the hide with a bone tool with a blade, Stands Sacred Woman was removing the flesh and gristle.

Jane asked eagerly, "May I do that, please?"

Stands Sacred Woman handed her the tool, guiding Jane's hand. "Next year, I will teach Winona the whole process. You, too, of course, Little Bird. See, over there is another hide. It has dried in the sun, and now I must scrape it longer to give it an even thickness. After that, we must turn it over and remove the hair with a scraper, and it becomes hard and stiff."

Jane knew finished buffalo skins were soft. "How do you make it soft?"

"I will soak it in water for a few days, then cure it by rubbing it with fats, liver, and red grass."

"When do you rub it all over with the rawhide string, Mother?" Winona asked.

Stands Sacred Woman smiled at her daughter. "That is the last step. Do you girls want to try scraping the other skin to make it even?"

Jane and Winona stood side by side, pulling and scraping, and learning, before next summer.

"My, Jane, how you have grown!" exclaimed Mrs. Clark.

Dressed in her best dress that was now too short, Jane sat ,the lake's edge with the women of Fort Snelling and the Mission House.

"Yes, ma'am," Jane answered politely, grateful to Mrs. Clark for not mentioning her chopped off hair.

The men and ladies of the fort, weary of the summer heat, had arrived for a picnic. Now the men were off hunting for ducks and geese and Jane was enjoying the soft conversation and pretty clothing of the women. Lucy Anne, adorned in baby finery, was being passed around, and Mrs. Stevens and Lucy were glad of the company.

Someone suggested they walk a bit, and as

they did, Jane, now watchful for wild foods, suddenly burst out, "There is a vine of the mdo!"

Everyone was startled, but they were astonished when Jane knelt on the ground, untangled a slender vine amongst the weeds, and began digging with her hands. "Look!" she said triumphantly. "I found a mdo! They taste like sweet potatoes! Red Cherry Woman taught me where to look for them."

Jane stood up triumphantly, the hem of her dress dusty, her hands covered with dirt. She dangled the vegetable from her fingers, looking to her friends for approval. She was met with silence.

In a strained voice, Mrs. Stevens said, "Jane, go wash your hands. A lady does not dig in the dirt in her good clothing."

There were other visits that summer, and Jane was always glad to see her fort friends, but there was more to learn in the village.

Once again the heat of summer subsided, and the trees and bushes were kissed with new color. Winona scampered up the cottonwood trunk ladder onto the watcher's stage, Jane just behind her. There they talked and played games, waiting until someone spied the hungry blackbirds. Harpen's field was nearby, so she joined them. Some birds landed. All three girls leaped to their feet, shouting and waving cloth, frightening the birds away.

The season of green corn was already past. In August Jane had helped Stands Sacred Woman gather some unripe ears. Most of these she boiled on the cob in a kettle. She also scraped some from the cob with her thumbnail, and cooked the corn with beans. Both were delicious.

As the autumn deepened, Jane joined Red Cherry Woman and others in the fields to harvest the ripened corn. Quickly, Jane pulled the ears off the drying stalk. If she helped, she would get some fresh meat to take to the Mission House, for some of the men were already hunting. Mrs. Stevens had agreed to let Jane harvest with the Dakota people in exchange for meat. She worked along happily, faster than Winona who was younger.

The corn stalks rattled a little in the breeze. The sky was a brilliant blue, with a few wispy clouds. Soon she would help gather the squash, as she had picked the beans. When she grew up, Jane vowed, she would garden, too.

Evening came on early now. Jane was walking back towards the Mission House, for it was time to help with supper, and Waa-bec was walking with her part of the way. From the trees near the lake's edge came the call of an owl.

Jane started.

Waa-bec looked at her curiously. "What is wrong?"

"That sound scares me," Jane said. She had a vague memory of someone else shivering at the sound of an owl. Mrs. Stevens? Jane's own mother?

"Why should it scare you? Owls are good birds, and very powerful. You should not fear the wild creatures, Jane. They are holy."

Jane was silent, listening again to the soft call, as if it were calling to her.

"The only fear is if you hear a screech owl. It will not harm you, but it may be telling you that someone is to die soon," Waa-bec said.

"Do you think an owl would know? And do you think an owl would tell you?" Jane asked.

"Of course," Waa-bec said. "My grandmother heard an owl call her father's name the night he died. Look!"

Waa-bec pointed towards the trees. The owl had risen from its perch in the trees and was soaring out over the lake. They watched until it was beyond the lake and they could see it no more.

Mrs. Stevens was peeling potatoes and Lucy was slicing onions when Jane came in.

"Waska's baby brother died last night," Jane said quietly. "He got sick a few days ago."

Mrs. Stevens rested her hands on the bowl of potatoes, and gazed into the fire.

"Babies die so easily, especially in this wilderness. Oh, I know how his mother feels! One never quite gets over losing a child," she said, as if to herself. Then she stood up. "Jane, I must do something for her. What do you think I should do?"

Jane shrugged, startled by Mrs. Stevens's strong feelings. Maybe Mrs. Stevens did like the Dakota women, but she was too shy to show it.

"Perhaps some food," Mrs. Stevens said, thinking aloud. "I do have everything I need for a cake. Jane, when it is finished, put on your good dress, wash your face, and take it over there."

When Jane arrived, she found Good Star Woman wrapping her baby's body in the embroidered cloth she had so lovingly made before he was born. Continuing to wrap it in more blankets, she cried, saying over and over, "Me choonk she! Me choonk she!"

Jane knew she was saying, "My child, my

child, my child...." Nearby, the baby's father began singing the mourning song, and soon Waska sang it, too. She did not sing with her father. So wrapped in her own grief, she sang at her own pace and pitch. Other relatives arrived and joined in, each in their own time. The whole lodge seemed filled with a desperate sadness.

When the baby's body was properly wrapped, Good Star Woman, still moaning and wailing, took a knife and cut off her long hair, to show her great sadness.

Jane laid the cake near the cooking fire, and left quietly. Soon the family would place the baby's body on a scaffold, too, where it would be safe until burial. They might leave the baby's cradleboard on the scaffold, too, for seeing it empty would be too much to bear. Good Star Woman might even cut her legs with the knife, for she believed that pain in her body would lessen the pain of her loss.

That evening, those in the Mission House could hear the mourning cries and songs of the baby's family. For hours, they went on, and seemed to seep into the cozy room, the sadness drifting and stretching to fill every corner with grief.

They were silent. Jane sat close by Mrs. Stevens who was sitting near the fire, quietly crying.

The firelight danced on the tioti walls as
Chief Cloud Man talked. Jane sat close to Winona,
Chaske, Harpen, Waska, and Waa-bec, listening to
every word. Even tiny We-harka joined the group.

"It is important that you young ones know
why we are here. For generations, our people have
fed themselves by hunting and gathering. We are
good hunters, and the spirits look kindly upon us,
giving us food. Still, there are times when the winters
are long, the hunting scarce, and we go hungry. We
do not want our children and our old people to suf-
fer, and so we work hard, but still, there are years
when hunger is with us.

"I am chief, and I must look to the future for
my grandchildren, and their grandchildren. I see the
ways of others coming, making it hard, even impossible, for us and our ways. Sometime ago, when you
children were but babies, I was with a hunting party
when a blizzard came upon us. For days, with only
whirling snow as my companion, I was alone with
my thoughts. We were in this difficulty because of
hunting. Perhaps to avoid this, we could plant more,
as Major Taliaferro has suggested. I decided that if I
survived this storm, I would be willing to try. So we
came here to learn to plow and plant greater gardens.

We will see, we will see...but we must be on our
guard, for here, our enemies are not so far away."

"Tell us of a battle," someone said.

The chief got to his feet and began drawing
scenes from a remarkable battle on the tioti lining,
for, he said, the children must know of their past.
The battle came alive to Jane through his words and
drawings.

"Our enemy had one hundred warriors, and
our warriors were very few, only eleven. But they
fought bravely and well, and in the end, there were
many of the enemy dead, and not one Dakota was
even wounded," he said. Pausing in his drawing, he
put his hand upon his mouth, a mark of wonder.
"The spirits looked favorably upon us that great
day."

"Another story, please?" Waa-bec ventured.

The adults smiled at one another. A story was
begun by Red Hawk, and the serious mood changed.

"It is said that there was once a young man
out hunting buffalo with his father. They were riding horses, and when they saw a buffalo in the distance, the father noticed the son was still wearing his
robe, which would make it difficult for him to shoot.
'You should take off your robe to shoot at it!' the
father called so the son could hear him over the

sounds of the running horses and buffalo. Right away, the young man reined in his horse, and as the buffalo escaped, the young man got off his horse. He laid his robe on the ground and shot it full of holes!"

Jane and the other children laughed. How could anyone be so foolish? We-harka clapped her baby hands, the fire danced, and the stories went on.

Rumor spread throughout the village that Chief Red Bird and some of his men were coming. They would hold a council with Cloud Man and other village men at the Mission House.

"Clear the big room of chairs and whatever can be carried out," the reverend directed Evert and Dwight. "Jane, come here."

When she stood before him, he looked at her, and said in a voice even more serious than usual, "Jane, this is an important meeting. I must understand what is being said. You will interpret. Listen well, and tell me everything they say."

In the evening, the large room was soon filled with important people who made themselves comfortable on the floor. Chief Red Bird sat with his men and Chief Cloud Man entered with his usual dignity.

Jane stood for the entire meeting in the center, listening intently, and translating for the reverend. The Dakota were concerned about the Ojibwa people, their enemies. Jane felt very grown-up with her interpreting job.

In the morning, however, she felt mischievous instead. She was up early with Mrs. Stevens and Lucy, who were preparing food for the many men who were still sleeping in the large room, rolled in their blankets on the floor.

As she stirred the biscuit batter, Jane remembered the day Gideon told her of the Dakota belief that a woman jumping over a man's feet meant he would never run fast again. She began to form a plan so silly she had to stifle a giggle. Jane slipped unseen into the big room. Quickly she began jumping over the feet of the blanketed forms on the floor.

One by one the men awoke to find the serious little girl of last night jumping over them and laughing as she did so. Grumblings and groanings, even a shout, woke Chief Red Bird. He sat up, watched for a moment, and began chuckling.

Lucy came to the door to usher Jane out, but by now, all were laughing at the brave little girl who had fooled them.

There were more council meetings at the

Mission House, attended by important men, including Chief Wabasha. Jane served as interpreter many times. Still, she was always watchful for a chance to jump over the feet of unsuspecting men!

It was time for the muskrat hunt and sugar bush camp. The snow was wet and melting in sun-warmed places, leaving muddy patches. Bringing in the milk from Gideon's cow, Jane paused outside, breathing in the air that was still winter, but promised spring.

Coming into the house, Jane saw the family gathered around Lucy who was reading a letter the reverend had brought back from the fort.

"Dear all," she read. "I have completed my studies and am now an ordained minister. As I want to serve the Dakota people, I will return to the Lake Harriet Mission, arriving sometime in May. I sincerely hope all is well with my many friends there. God's blessings to you, Samuel Pond."

Jane set the milk pail down. She wanted to jump up and down, but the reverend seemed less than joyful himself, and the family was quiet. So she said a prayer that Samuel would have a safe trip, and be back with her soon.

She had swept out the little cabin, and washed the window. Now she wiped clean the table where Samuel ate and wrote.

"I missed you, Miss Jane—or should I say 'Little Bird'?" Samuel said, his warm smile spreading over his face. "I thought of you often, and prayed for you."

"Me, too," Jane said shyly.

Samuel went on, "I hope you are not disappointed that I will not live in the Mission House. That was too difficult. For a year, I have studied in English. I missed speaking Dakota. Sit down now, and tell me all you have learned of Dakota life while I was away—but first, let me get my ink and quill. You probably know words I want to add to my lists."

The Dakota men were plowing the cornfields, and planting had begun. Samuel worked with them, they marveling at his willingness to do women's work, he marveling at how well they now gardened.

Jane was hoeing the young corn plants with Red Cherry Woman when Samuel paused to greet them. Lucy Anne was playing nearby with We-harka.

"That is quite a helpful grandchild you have there, Red Cherry Woman," Samuel called.

Red Cherry Woman straightened up and

smiled at Samuel. "My 'takoja', Little Bird, learns fast and well," she said.

"Mrs. Stevens sent this cornbread for you," Jane said when Samuel answered her knock on his door. She and Winona stood there, hoping to be invited in. They were not disappointed.

Samuel had paper, ink bottles, his Bible, and several quill pens on his table.

"What are you doing, Grizzly Bear?" Winona asked.

"Writing a story from the Bible, putting it into Dakota. It will be the first Bible story written in your language, I believe. Do you know the story of Joseph, the boy with eleven jealous brothers?"

Winona shook her head.

"I have heard it, but never in Dakota," Jane said.

"Well, sit down then, for you are in for a good story," Samuel said.

"Do you know what those men are building, Mr. Pond?" Jane asked Samuel one day as they walked through the village.

They stopped to look at a small, dome-shaped frame built of willow poles. Some of the villagers

were placing buffalo robes over the frame so it would be airtight.

"Yes. It is a sweat lodge, a very special place," Samuel explained. "When a Dakota man hopes to have a vision or to somehow gain wisdom or power from the spirits, he must purify himself. It will be very hot and steamy inside and the men will smoke tobacco together. It is all done very carefully, and in a certain order. When they are finished, the men who participate will be ready to receive a vision."

Jane watched as the builders struggled to place the robes just right.

"Do women ever use the sweat lodge?" Jane asked.

"No, Little Bird. It is not believed they need to, for the life-bringers are already strong and holy," Samuel said. "Do you know Holy Door Woman?"

Jane nodded. That was We-harka's grandmother.

"She is called that because it is often her job to sit outside the door of the sweat lodge—the door always faces east, by the way—and pray for the men inside."

They watched quietly, and then Samuel said, "I never tire of learning about the ways the people here live. It is not my way, but I ask myself, is it right for me to judge?"

She looked up at his face and saw how intently he was watching the sweat lodge being built. They remained silent.

It was autumn. Soon Jane would be nine years old. She helped her friends with the harvest again, as well as worked to gather food from the

Stevenses' garden. She cared for Lucy Ann easily now. She was almost two years old and Jane was quite grown up.

October brought the hunt. Jane watched as Samuel and the villagers left, wishing she could go, too. Still, this winter would not be as lonely as the last, for Mrs. Stevens had announced one day, letter in hand, that her sister, Miss Cordelia Eggleston, would arrive soon to help Lucy in school. Everyone was glad of this news, especially Mrs. Stevens.

Jane suspected that there would be another newcomer, though no one ever mentioned it. Mrs. Stevens was growing rounder. Jane was sure a new baby was coming.

An old white dress had been ripped and made into curtains. The room upstairs that had been Gideon's was now made ready for Miss Cordelia. She arrived with great energy and a great trunk. The Mission House was alive with her arrival.

There were new dresses for Mrs. Stevens, and dresses to be made over for Jane. Miss Cordelia cooed over Lucy Anne, delighted in how tall Evert and Dwight had become, exclaimed over the wilderness, and asked questions about the Dakota people. And she had brought new song books for the school.

She would work with Lucy for at least a year.

As Christmas approached, Samuel returned from the hunt with many stories. Those were happy nights in the Mission House as they all gathered to listen to Samuel's tales.

"This time I was more comfortable—or rather less uncomfortable— than in the winter of 1835. We had not bread nor salt, but plenty of good food. Fortunately for me, my gun was broken early on, and that excused me from going hunting each day. I could stay in the camp, where I heard much language, the hunt I was truly on. When the men hunt, they are, of course, silent. In camp, it is the opposite! When I wanted to be alone, I had my pocket Testament with me, and also a lexicon in Greek."

"You are a devotee of languages, Mr. Pond?" Miss Cordelia asked.

"Yes, ma'am. I have studied Greek. I am also interested in the way cultures of long ago can mirror today's cultures."

Cordelia nodded, greatly interested. "And you are also an ordained minister?"

Samuel said he was. Reverend Stevens shifted in his chair, crossing his arms across his chest.

"Where did you sleep, sir?" Dwight asked, briefly glancing at his father first. "When you were on the hunt?"

"I stayed with a family, a middle-aged man, Hehan Maza, or Iron Owl, his wife, and his two nephews. The men were all good hunters, so there was always venison enough for us all. He estimated the number of deer that I ate, and I paid him. He and his wife never claimed I owed them anything for all they did for me. The Dakota are remarkable. They do not think they should store up riches, and they always are ready to share. They actually have a very Christian attitude in many ways."

"But they are not Christians—none of these people you speak of?" Cordelia asked.

"No, we have not had any conversions. They have their own way of seeing life and God, one that I am struggling to understand," Samuel said. "I will tell you a funny story now. One rather warm day, I was coming down from the north with Badger, Waabec's father. It was thawing, so we were wading through the melting snow, sometimes up to our knees in water. Suddenly, Badger stopped and burst out laughing loudly. I was quite startled by this, for Badger is usually a quiet man. Of course, I asked him what was so funny. 'I was thinking what a fool you are to be here wading in this melting snow when you might be at home in a comfortable house with plenty of good food,' he said. That got me to thinking. Many a white man would, no doubt, have called me a fool, too. But not many would have laughed so hard as they stood up to their knees in cold water!"

Samuel laughed at the memory.

Cordelia looked thoughtfully at Samuel and said, "You truly respect these people, and want to learn all their ways."

Samuel stopped laughing, but his eyes were still merry as he answered, "Yes, Miss Cordelia. I do."

There was a knock at the Mission House door on a snowy December afternoon. Jane answered to find a Frenchman wearing snowshoes.

Cordelia was called, for she spoke French.

"He has come a long way on these snowshoes, from a place called Lac qui Parle. He says he has letters for you," she translated.

The letters were from Dr. Williamson, who wrote of news from his mission, and from Sarah.

Jane listened as Mrs. Stevens read aloud the first letter. It was the second that caught her real attention.

"Sarah is married!" Mrs. Stevens said. "She is

married to Gideon Pond!"

Dwight and Jane exchanged surprised glances. Then Jane felt a terrible disappointment. This, she was sure, meant that Gideon would never come back.

"It is 1838!" Lucy said one frigid morning. "I wonder what this new year will bring!"

Not many days later, the new year brought the new baby, a boy. He was named Aaron, for he was born in the wilderness, where the biblical Aaron had lived.

Jane and Lucy Anne went up to the bedroom to see him. Lucy Anne clung to Jane's hand. She did not smile, but said in her two-year-old way, "He is little."

"Yes," Jane said wisely. "As little as you were once, but you grew. I suppose he will, too!"

With January, the deep cold set in, and smoke curled from the tipi as the Dakota women dragged home more wood for the next day's fire. They banked snow up around each tioti for insulation. It was a quiet scene that might seem sad, but Jane knew the restful time for the Dakota was here. Stories were being told, clothing sewn and decorated.

It was a time of closeness and creativity.

Still, one cold, cold winter day, Harpen came to the Mission House with a large piece of rawhide.

"Little Bird, can you come sliding?" she asked.

It was not quiet in the village that afternoon.

The ground was muddy and soggy as Jane, with Lucy Anne in tow, walked to Samuel's cabin. He had a letter he wanted to share with the people at the Mission House. Jane had come to fetch it.

"It is from Gideon. He has been working hard on translating the Bible into Dakota," Samuel announced. "He and a man named Joseph Renville, who speaks French, are working on it. Renville reads the Bible in French, then translates it out loud into Dakota, and Gideon writes it down in Dakota, using our alphabet. They have two of the gospels translated already! Little Bird, this is good news indeed! We can begin to truly tell the Dakota people of Jesus! Perhaps, God willing, they will become believers!"

Jane saw the light in Samuel's eyes, but she was confused. Were not the Dakota people believers already? She thought of the many times she had heard Stands Sacred Woman say a prayer of thanksgiving as she prepared food, of Chief Cloud Man's prayers before a hunt, of the offering she saw on the boulders. They believed in God, in their own way.

Samuel went on, "Gideon writes of an attack on the Dakota where he is, which is certainly disturbing news. But there is good news, too! He is coming for a long visit with his wife and baby daughter!"

Letter in hand, Jane trudged back to the Mission House with Lucy Anne. Gideon was a papa! And he and Sarah were coming to visit!

With Cordelia here, another school was started. The reverend was excited about this school, and Jane was, too, for several girls were coming from Fort Snelling to live at the Mission House or in the village and go to Cordelia's school.

"Mary Taliaferro is coming to school here. You would call her my cousin, but I call her my sister. She lives at the fort right now," Winona told Jane.

Mary? Jane thought that did not sound like a Dakota name. And Taliaferro. "Is she the major's daughter?" Jane asked.

Winona nodded.

"Then how can she be your cousin?" Jane

asked.

"Because her mother, The Day Sets, is my mother's sister."

Jane thought about this for a minute. Then she ventured, "Winona, where is your father?"

Winona turned her lovely, dark eyes to Jane, smiling gently. She was, Jane thought, as beautiful as her mother.

"My father's name is Seth Eastman. He was a soldier and an artist at the fort. Many of the soldiers there marry Dakota women, and he married my mother. When I was a baby, he had to go away to another fort. It is not the Dakota way for my mother and me to leave our family, so we stayed here."

"Do you ever see him?"

"No, he and my mother are not married now. But my mother and grandmother told me that he loved me very much, and was very sad to leave me."

Jane thought of the man who was her father, far away and long ago. "Do you miss your father?"

"I do not remember him, Little Bird. But I have my family here."

The girls walked to the school, where they found Cordelia unpacking books. Samuel was helping her, and they seemed to be laughing. They stopped when Jane and Winona came in.

"Hello!" Samuel greeted them. "I hear, Winona, that you will be in this class when the girls from the fort arrive."

She nodded and smiled. "My sister will come, too. And my other mother, The Day Sets, will be here also. We will be glad to have them in the village."

Jane listened, but she watched, too.

Back at the Mission House, as she rocked

Seth Eastmen

Aaron she said to Lucy, who was setting the table for supper, "I saw Mr. Pond and Miss Cordelia laughing and talking in the schoolroom today."

"Hush," Lucy said. "Do not poke your nose into other people's business."

Gideon looked cheerful and baby Ruth fit perfectly into his arms. Sarah smiled a great deal. Somehow she seemed stronger now.

It was a happy time in the Mission House, and in the village as well, for the Dakota people were glad to see Gideon and meet his wife and daughter.

One day Lucy asked Jane to run over to the school for she wanted a book to show Sarah. Jane slipped into the building, assuming it was empty, but found the Pond brothers talking earnestly together. They did not hear her come in.

"Has it improved any?" Gideon asked.

"It has with the Dakota people, though I have not had any converts yet. I appreciate them more each day, though I find their way of life so demanding. But Stevens? He says he respects me as a minister, but he is stubborn, and unwilling to do anything my way. And he is not especially liked by the people here. He has not only not converted anyone, but he has led some to dislike him, which does not help our cause."

"It is better for me," Gideon said. "Dr. Williamson is a good man. And he is much easier to work with. And of course, I am happy with Sarah, too. We talk of our own mission at another location, and we want you to come with us, Samuel. Leave here, and 'shake the dust from your feet,' as scripture tells us."

"Yes," Samuel said. "The time may come for that. We will speak again of this."

Jane picked up the book Lucy wanted, and walked slowly back to the Mission House, which no longer seemed like a happy place.

"Jane, will you take care of Ruth?" Sarah asked her one summer day. "Gideon and I are going on a picnic!"

Winona joined her. She and Jane laid a blanket in the shade just outside the Mission House, and brought Ruth and Aaron outside. Lucy Anne skipped along, happy to be considered a big girl.

They heard the hoof beats of an approaching horse.

"That looks like the reverend," Winona said, peering into the distance.

"It could be," Jane said. "He preached at the fort yesterday, and is expected back today."

It was the reverend, and when he rode up he barely tethered his horse before storming into the house.

"Wife! Julia!" he called. "I have bad news. Remember I told you that Major Taliaferro was told by the government to appoint a farmer for each band of Indians?"

"Of course, Jedediah, and you applied for the position here," Mrs. Stevens replied.

"Well, I just learned he has appointed one, and it is not I. It is Samuel Pond."

Jane and Winona looked at each other. Winona did not understand most of the English, and Jane did not understand the meaning.

"Well, Jedediah, perhaps it is for the best. You are a minister, not a farmer. And Mr. Pond, though he is ordained, is a good farmer."

"You do not understand!" the reverend shouted. "I have been here two-and-a-half years and I have not made any progress as far as the church is concerned. What if the ministry board dismisses me?"

"This is a difficult mission. The board knows that, Jedediah. Do not worry unnecessarily, dear husband," Mrs. Stevens said.

Jane stood up and saw that down by the lake, Gideon and Sarah were walking with Samuel and someone else. It was a woman, and Samuel was holding her arm. Who was it?

Cordelia.

Jane sat down, and rubbed Aaron's back. She did not understand all that grown-ups said and did.

The August heat was oppressive, so Waa-bec came looking for swimmers. Jane and Evert joined the others. Dwight no longer swam with them. He said he was too old now.

The others climbed aboard some logs and paddled out into the lake. Splash! Chaske sent a wave of water all over Jane. Then Waa-bec shouted, "Look! Something is wrong."

Some villagers had gathered, talking excitedly. Samuel was there, too. When the children reached shore, Samuel came towards them.

"What has happened, Mr. Pond?" Evert asked, his clothes dripping onto the dusty ground beneath him.

"I have just told the villagers that when I was at the fort yesterday, some Ojibwa men were shot and killed just outside of it. Most likely it was done by Dakota from another village."

Jane shivered, despite the heat.

"What does this mean?" Evert asked.

"It means to me that some men are needlessly dead, and their families must grieve and get along without them," Samuel said. "And it means that the Dakota people will have to be on the look-out, for when something like this happens, there is usually revenge."

Jane looked back at the excited group near the bark lodges.

"Come, Jane," Evert said. "We must go home and change out of these wet clothes."

"I will go with you to inform Mr. Stevens," Samuel said.

They walked in silence the rest of the way.

Most of the villagers had left for the hunt, but the girls who attended Cordelia's school remained. Lucy's twenty students were gone, so she joined Cordelia.

Gideon, Sarah, and their child lived in the small Pond cabin. Samuel was gone on the hunt, as was his custom. But he said he would be back earlier than last year. Cordelia had smiled and blushed when he said that, and Lucy had said stoutly, "Of course you will be back in November, Samuel Pond!"

One day in late October, the wind whipping her skirt around her ankles, Jane asked Dwight if Samuel and Cordelia were getting married.

"I guess so," Dwight said, disgust in his voice. "But nobody tells me anything around here."

Dwight went on to fetch firewood, and Jane, milk pail in hand, went into the house. A wedding! Samuel was getting married!

"A little to the left, Evert," Mrs. Stevens said. "Jane, help him fasten those branches to the walls."

Lucy looked over the pile of tamarack and cedar boughs on the table. "You and Dwight chose beautiful branches, Evert. These will be wonderful decorations for the wedding. This is so exciting!" she said, then sighing romantically, she added, "And to think it will be on Cordelia's twenty-third birthday!"

"Now children," Mrs. Stevens said distractedly. "There will be distinguished guests here for the wedding. You must be polite to everyone. Good gracious, Lucy, do not let the bread burn!"

The great day arrived. Outside the Mission House the jolly sound of sleigh bells tinkled in the air as twilight came on. The big room was soon filled with ladies and gentlemen from the fort, including Major Taliaferro.

"Look, they have pretty flowers in their hair!" Lucy Anne said to Jane.

The ladies were dressed in their best, and Lucy Anne was quite starry eyed. She and Jane stood together, near the door of the great room.

The reverend was standing at the other end, looking a bit uncomfortable. He was wearing his Sunday coat. Sarah, Gideon, and Mrs. Stevens sat near him. The guests found seats and chatted.

A bell sounded, and everyone hushed. Jane felt excitement hovering in the room.

The door opened. Jane saw Samuel, looking handsome in a good suit, with his friend, Henry Sibley, from the fort. Jane gazed at Samuel. He seemed very solemn, but for a moment, he glanced at Jane. His familiar smile warmed his face, and she smiled back at him. Then he and Henry stepped slowly to the front of the room.

All attention was focused on the empty doorway where two young women appeared. "So pretty!" Lucy Anne whispered, and Jane nodded. They walked side by side, Cordelia dressed all in white, a lacy veil on her head. Lucy was in white, too, with pink ribbons on the lace on her shoulders. When Samuel and Cordelia stood next to each other, the reverend read from his prayer book. The room was quiet, and a prayer was said. Then happy congratulations and conversation filled the room. The feast began, but Jane's job was to stay out of the way, with Lucy Anne. Even Dwight and Evert were told to watch from the stairs.

Still, they enjoyed the party, and when Jane went up to her bedroom, she was surprised to feel that it was much colder than usual. She had not realized that a storm had begun. Hard snowflakes pinged against the window, and the wind seemed to be shaking the house. She crawled into bed. Before

she slept, she wondered how Waa-Bec and Winona
were faring in their tipi, out on the hunt.

In the morning, Jane carried plates of hot-
cakes to the guests, who had been snowed in. There
was much laughter and talk. A few hours later, the
sleighs were brought to the Mission House. Jane and
Lucy Anne watched as warm buffalo robes were
tucked around the heavily dressed travelers. They
heard calls of gratitude and good-byes.

Several of the women turned and waved their
fur muffs toward the schoolhouse, and the men
saluted towards it.

"Why do they wave?" Lucy Anne asked.

Jane peered at the school.

There, in the upstairs window, were Cordelia
and Samuel.

That, Jane realized, was their new home.

The reverend left a week after the wedding.
He was traveling south on horseback to Chief
Wabasha's village to talk with them about farming.

Jane was not sure why he left, except that he
was worried about something called the ministry
board. They might not want him to work at the
Lake Harriet Mission anymore. She knew that others
had advised him not to travel so far in the winter,

but he held firm.

He said good-bye, mounted his horse, and rode off on a day so sunny it hurt Jane's eyes to look at the glittering snow.

Leaving Home, Again

Chapter Seven

He had not returned. Christmas had come
and gone, a new year had begun. Baby
Aaron had his first birthday. The winter
blizzards raged, and the March thaws followed. The

villagers left for the sugar bush camp or muskrat hunting. But there was no word or sign of the reverend.

Mrs. Stevens was silent. Lucy prepared all the meals and took care of Aaron as she watched Mrs. Stevens gazing out of the window. She told Jane and the boys to do all they could to help out. No one spoke of him anymore at the Mission House.

Others, however, did talk of him. In the village, Jane heard speculation that winter-hungry wolves might have attacked him. Some of their friends from the fort stopped by, and said to Samuel, "A foolhardy trip in winter..."

The Ponds were kind and helpful, but as spring spread across the prairie, there was very little hope in the Mission House.

One day in April, Mrs. Stevens was rocking Aaron when she called to Jane.

"Take the baby. There is an old man walking down by the lake shore. He may be lost, for he looks very weak. For the sake of my husband, I want to go and help him," she said, pulling her shawl around her shoulders.

Jane positioned the chunky baby on her hip. He tugged at her shoulder-length hair, but Jane hardly noticed, for the scene by the lake took all her attention.

Mrs. Stevens approached the man, then threw her arms around him. Jane could hear her voice, high and excited, then saw her supporting him, bringing him to the Mission House.

"Oh my husband! Where have you been?" Mrs. Stevens was saying.

Could this be the reverend? Jane drew back, a little frightened. This man with hollow cheeks and matted hair? This man, who looked so much older than the reverend?

"Jane, get him some milk, right away! Then find Lucy. Tell her to prepare some venison broth! Find the boys, too, after you get the food."

For several days the reverend rested in a darkened room. Finally, he was able to sit in a chair to tell his story.

"I was on my way to see Chief Wabasha when I lost my way. I wandered about the woods until my horse and I were worn out. I sensed I was going in circles, and I gave up in despair. I abandoned my horse, and sat down where I wrote out the whole story in the margins of my Bible. In it I said my good-byes to all of you. And then I lay down to die. I slept from exhaustion, but awoke to find I was being carried in a blanket to someone's tioti. The Indians there fed me well, sharing their food of dried meat and corn. I was given warm buffalo skins to sleep on, and the fire was kept going so I was comfortable. They gave me medicines, and cared for me tenderly. The men even went out and found my Bible for me, and looked for the horse, but it was never found. When I thought the weather would permit it, I began walking back here. The Indians, heathens though they are, were very kind to me."

Mrs. Pond wrote the date on the board: May 9, 1839.

Sitting on her bench, Jane looked at all the girls who were her friends, and at Cordelia, book in hand, ready to help children learn. Jane felt a lump in her throat. She did not want to leave here.

When he was stronger, the reverend had traveled to the fort, and had come home jubilant. His announcement had made Jane anything but happy.

"I had a meeting with Major Taliaferro," he explained. "He has agreed to give me the appointment of farmer to Wabasha's band! It is not certain when we will leave yet, but the appointment is official."

Outside, the grasses and trees by the lake

were greening. Birds sang
everywhere. Life was busy in
the bark lodges. Jane gazed
out the window and won-
dered how much longer she
would be a part of it.

The June day dawned hot, and as Jane
brought in the pail of milk she met Evert with the
water bucket.

"It is so hot already," Jane said, wiping a
strand of hair from her forehead. "Let's ask Waa-bec
if he wants to swim today"

Evert shook his head. "I just saw Waa-bec. He
and his uncle, Beaver, are leaving for the day to hunt.
Waa-bec was excited because his father told him if he
kills a bird today, he will be given a gun."

Pouring the milk into the milk pans, Jane
wondered about Waa-bec. If a boy owns a gun, would
he still want to play in the lake and eat turtle soup?

Jane stepped out into the hot sunshine.
Someone was running toward the village. It was
Waa-bec, and he was running faster than ever before.
Perhaps he had killed his bird, and he wanted to tell
everyone he would now get a gun. She started for the

village, hoping to be in on Waa-bec's news. As she drew closer, she saw that Waa-bec's grin was gone. He began shouting, and Dakota men and women came running. Something was very wrong.

She was about to join them when Gideon stepped out of a lodge. He saw Jane and gestured to her to go away. Confused, she obeyed. Walking slowly back to the Mission House, she stopped frequently to look back.

The group around Waa-bec was growing larger and more excited. Gideon broke away from them, hurrying towards the Mission House. He soon caught up with her.

"Are Sarah and Ruth still at the Mission House?" he asked. "Yes. They are with Lucy and Cordelia, Jane said. "Everyone is there today, even the reverend."

"Good. I must find Samuel. Go into the house and tell them to stay there until Samuel and I come. Do not leave the house, Jane. No one must leave," he said, then veered off in search of Samuel.

They were waiting anxiously in the large room when Gideon and Samuel entered.

Gideon spoke immediately. "Beaver has been killed. He was ambushed by some Ojibwa warriors.

The boy, Waa-bec, was in the tall grass, so he was not found nor harmed. As soon as he knew he was alone, Waa-bec ran back to the village. It happened not far from here. The Ojibwa may be near and could attack at any moment, or they may be satisfied with one death. The villagers are meeting now to decide if they will ambush the Ojibwa."

Jane stood next to Cordelia, and a feeling of dread came over her. Waa-bec could easily have been killed this morning! And his uncle, whom Waa-bec so loved, lay dead. She shuddered and Cordelia put her arm around her shoulder.

Sarah, holding Ruth close, said, "Oh, Gideon, this is just like at Lac qui Parle! Why must they fight?"

It was Samuel who answered quietly, "They have enemies. What group of people doesn't? If we whites did not have enemies, would we have armies? And who amongst us does not have ancestors from Europe who fought for land rights? That is really what is happening here. The Ojibwa and Dakota people are both fighting to maintain their hunting lands. If one group ever takes over, the other group perishes."

"Can't something be done at Fort Snelling to settle these disputes?" Lucy asked.

"It is not possible for our government to convince each Indian group to respect the others and hunt only in certain areas. And do you think, if the Dakota complained to the fort commandant that Ojibwa hunters were on Dakota land, that the commandant would be successful in settling it? The conflicts go back much further than any fort commandant," Gideon said.

"But what about Chief Cloud Man?" Cordelia asked. "Have you spoken with him, Samuel?"

"He feels war begets war, attack only invites attack," Samuel answered.

"But Dakota government is democratic. A chief, no matter how good a leader, cannot control the final decision. And I am afraid the final decision will be war. Many of the villagers feel Beaver's death must be avenged," Gideon said.

The reverend now spoke up. His voice sounded small and hollow. He said, "But they will bring back scalps."

"I am afraid so, Mr. Stevens," Samuel said. "We must expect it. But are scalps of dead enemies any different from an epaulet or sword a white soldier has taken from an enemy soldier he has just killed? And the badges of honor they receive——are the soldiers who earn these unlike the Dakota warriors who want glory in battle?"

"Are you saying, Mr. Pond, that this killing that may happen here is right?" Lucy asked.

"I am not saying it is right, Miss Lucy. I am just saying it may not be different from wars fought by white men," Samuel answered. "There is always the question of whether or not a war is right."

Just then, mourning cries rose from the village, much louder than Jane had ever heard before. She went over to the window. She could see We-harka's mother, wailing.

Gideon came over to her, glanced out the window and said, "Come with me, Jane. We need not see their unhappiness."

He led her away from the window. The wails rose higher.

"I want to go to the village," Jane cried out.

If Red Cherry Woman or Stands Sacred Woman needed her, she wanted to be there. She wanted to cry for Beaver, too. What if the Ojibwa warriors came back for Waa-bec? What if Winona got hurt? Maybe Jane could help.

"No," Samuel said gently but firmly. "It is dangerous for everyone right now. You must stay here, Jane."

Gideon pulled her onto his lap. As a cry arose from the village, he tenderly drew Jane's head to his chest and covered her ears. She could feel his heart beating.

Life seemed very fragile at that moment.

The babies and Lucy Anne slept in the arms of adults, but no one else slept that long, long night.

They were waiting for an attack. None came, but the mourning cries continued for hours.

Jane was dozing next to Lucy, when Gideon quietly left the house in the early morning. He returned with news.

"During the night Chief Cloud Man met with his men and a decision has been made. They will attack an Ojibwa village. Some men from Red Bird's village are coming here to join them. There should be at least a hundred warriors. I expect they will leave here near sundown," he reported. He ran his hand through his hair. Jane thought he looked tired and discouraged. "At least there will not be any fighting right here."

"For the time being," Sarah added quietly.

Gideon looked at her, sighed, but said nothing more.

"What do we do now?" Mrs. Stevens asked, her face white with exhaustion.

"Wait," Samuel said. "And pray."

"And stay inside," the reverend added. "Do not allow any of the children outside today."

When it was nearing sundown, Jane remembered that the warriors would leave then. She slipped upstairs to look out the window where no adults could notice her.

The village was quiet, and this disturbed her. Then she saw movement near the distant cornfields. She realized she was seeing the warriors silently leaving on their way to do battle.

The quiet continued. Tension was running high in the Mission House. Then a shout and glad cries filled the air. The village seemed alive again, this time with a wild, joyful fervor. Those in the Mission House ran to the village.

Jane's heart pounded as she saw Winona, Harpen, and Chaske gathered there. Waa-bec stood with his mother, his face a mixture of excitement, sadness, and exhaustion.

They were clustered around a warrior of Red Bird's village, who had come back as a runner. They had been successful, he said. Soon the warriors would be returning with seventy scalps. Beaver's death was avenged!

Fascinated, Jane watched as both the women and men of the village danced the scalp dance. Weharka's grandmother raised the long pole on which the scalps had been hung. The other women formed a circle around her, dressed in their best,

their blankets wrapped around their shoulders. They stood close together, very straight, their eyes fixed on the ground.

The drum began, the voices were raised in the song sung only for the scalp dance. The women moved together in a circle to the beat of the drum, singing as they did so.

Men joined the dance, and Jane noticed that their movements were not as smooth as the women's. Sometimes they formed two lines, the men facing the women. They would dance towards each other, then move back again.

The song had only a few words, which were repeated over and over, stamping themselves forever into Jane's mind. Sometimes the women would call out short, shrill notes, and the men would add their loud, defiant voices. The song was heard at the Mission House and far, far out onto the prairie.

Emotion was running high in the village, for there was joy at the success of their warriors, yet many people were mourning Beaver, and everyone was aware that a return attack could come at any minute.

Stands Sacred Woman, usually calm, was jumpy and distraught. Harpen looked over her shoulder as she talked with Jane. Chief Cloud Man seemed troubled. The young men talked of their bravery.

Still, life went on, gardens were tended to, babies were fed, children played.

As the summer days slipped by, the children

played the scalp dance over and over. That it meant
the death of others no longer occurred to Jane as she
danced and sang on the shores of Lake Harriet, and
when she tumbled exhausted into her bed at night,
the words of the scalp dance rang in her imagination.

"Samuel?" Jane asked. "What does it mean 'to
be dismissed'?"

Samuel looked up from his work. He now had
a collection of three thousand Dakota words for his
dictionary, and he had begun a grammar book, too.

"To be let go. You get dismissed from school
each day, Little Bird."

"How can the reverend be dismissed?"

"Ah, that is what I thought you might mean.
Reverend Stevens and I work for a missionary board,
a group of people who advise us and decide about
where we should work. The board has not been
happy with Mr. Stevens's work here, Jane. He has
been dismissed. He no longer works for the missionary board. In fact, I do not think he will work as a
minister."

"Why?"

"He has not had much success with the
Dakota people. He has not learned their language,
and he has had many arguments with others about

their work."

"Like you and Gideon?"

"Yes, but there were several others, too."

Samuel looked at her with searching eyes.

"That is why we are moving away?"

"Yes, that is why. And I will miss you terribly, Miss Jane. You are truly a little bird that was caught. I will always remember you."

Mrs. Stevens and Lucy were packing up. Still, they did not make Jane stay to help. She was allowed to go to Stands Sacred Woman's lodge. There she found Red Cherry Woman packing, too.

"Grandmother, is it time for the hunt already?" Jane asked.

"Almost, Little Bird, but we are leaving early. My husband is concerned that we here are too far from other Dakota encampments. We must be closer to other Dakota, after last summer's fighting. We have been fortunate that no attack has come yet, but it will. It will come sometime. We will be safer if we have settled closer to others we trust. Everyone of this village will move away."

"Stands Sacred Woman and Winona will go with you?"

"Of course."

"Will Waa-bec and Chaske and..."

"We will all leave, little one. There will no longer be a village here."

"Will you move to where Reverend Stevens is taking us?" Jane asked hopefully.

"No, we must say good-bye soon," Red Cherry Woman said gently. She stroked Jane's short braids. "Little Bird That Was Caught, I hope you fly free someday."

Jane had folded her apron and her work dress and placed them in the trunk when she found the book Mrs. Clark had given her. Soon it would be time to pass it on to Lucy Anne.

Under the book, she found the little doll she had made long ago with Red Cherry Woman's help. Lucy Anne was old enough for it now. Jane was glad Lucy Anne would have something from the place where she had been born.

Chief Cloud Man came to the Mission House to say good-bye. He met Jane outside.

Smiling, he placed his hands on her head. "Always remember, Little Bird, that the Dakota people are your friends."

The wagon was loaded, the door to the cozy

Mission House closed. Jane sat in the wagon. It was more crowded this time, for there were two more children than when they had arrived. Still, they were only going as far as Fort Snelling, where they would take a steamboat down the Mississippi River. Lucy Anne snuggled close to Jane, for it was chilly. They both held their Dakota dolls.

There had been one last argument between the reverend and the Pond brothers. Samuel had suggested the reverend leave his family at the fort until a suitable home could be built near Wabasha's village.

"No," the reverend said. "They are coming with me right now."

"But it is fall, winter will soon be here," Gideon pointed out. "Such young children cannot take winter without warm housing!"

"I can provide for my family, sir," the reverend said icily.

"Think of your experience last year, when you were lost and starving in the woods!" Samuel urged.

Jane saw the reverend's jaw was set as if it were made of stone. "They will come with me now."

And so it was time to leave. All the good-byes had been said, for the villagers had left for hunting and gathering. A site for a new village had been chosen on the Minnesota River, six miles upstream from Fort Snelling.

The Pond family gathered near the wagon. Jane knew they, too, would soon be moving. Now they stood together outside of the Mission House, waving and wishing everyone good luck.

"God go with you!" Samuel called to everyone in the wagon, but his eyes were on Jane.

The wagon started off, rolling past the silent bark lodges of Winona, Waa-bec, Chaske, We-harka, and the others.

It rolled on, once again taking Jane from her home.

Epilogue

"Little Bird That Was Caught" did eventually fly free, but she never forgot her Dakota friends.

The years after she left Lake Harriet were very difficult. Living conditions were extremely harsh at Wabasha's village, present-day Winona, Minnesota. Jane and the Stevens family survived hunger, theft, threats, wolves, and a prairie fire. Wabasha's people there were not interested in farming so, again unsuccessful, Reverend Stevens took the family into Wisconsin Territory. In three years they lived in four towns before moving to Elizabeth, Illinois, where Julia Stevens died after giving birth to another daughter. Jane planted flowers at her grave. Reverend Stevens remarried and moved his family to still another Illinois town. Jane, now in her late teens, chose to stay in Elizabeth.

There she met Heman Gibbs, a school teacher and farmer from Vermont. They were married in November, 1848, when Jane was twenty years old. Heman wanted to join the California Gold Rush, but the newlyweds decided instead to settle in the newly created Territory of Minnesota. Once again, Jane traveled up the Mississippi River. Heman purchased the land north of the pioneer village of St. Paul in

Jane as a bride

Rose Township, a part of present day Ramsey County. Their home still stands there as the Gibbs Farm Museum, owned by the Ramsey County Historical Society. Heman constructed a log-walled and sod-roofed half-underground dugout shanty where they lived for nearly five years. They had five children, four by birth and one by adoption. Their frame house was begun in 1854 and enlarged in the 1860s and 1870s. Jane finally had a permanent home. There they farmed and lived the rest of their lives.

Jane did return to New York to visit her family. She, Heman, and baby daughter Abbie traveled there in 1856. Jane's mother had died soon after Jane left with the Stevens family, never knowing that Jane was gone. Her father had also died. She found that he had tried to find her when he first learned of her leaving and that he had followed the Stevens wagon into Ohio before turning back. Her brothers and sisters were astonished to see Jane again, for they had thought her to be dead. They corresponded with Jane after that, and in 1890 Jane visited once more, with her daughter Lillie.

Gideon Pond

Gideon Pond and his family settled at Oak Grove, now Bloomington, Minnesota. This was the new location of Cloud Man's village after he left Lake Calhoun. Oak Grove was on the Minnesota River, about six miles up the river from Fort Snelling.

Samuel Pond

Samuel Pond and his family established a mission station at Shakopee, Minnesota, twenty-five miles west of Oak Grove. The last battle between the Dakota and Ojibwa bands, the Battle of Shakopee, took place nearby in May, 1858. Gideon Pond became a minister in 1848. Both Sarah and Cordelia died fairly young, and each brother remarried. They continued their work with the Dakota people and their language, watching as white settlement forced the Dakota into more and more difficult circumstances.

By 1851 the Ponds were disheartened, feeling the government policies that affected the Dakota people had made the missionaries' work impossible. The Ponds then founded and served churches for white settlers. Gideon continued this work until his death in January, 1878. Samuel retired and began writing about his experiences with the Dakota, their culture and language. He died in December, 1891. While neither was successful in converting any of the Dakota people to Christianity, both were extremely successful in teaching others about the Dakota way of life through their sharp and impartial observances, and their preservation of the Dakota language.

Stands Sacred Woman married a Dakota man and in 1851 was listed as living in Cloud Man's village in Oak Grove. Winona grew up to be a young woman of great beauty and soul, and was loved for her kindness, friendliness, and generosity. She was given the

name, Wakantankawin, or Great Spirit
Woman, a name no other Dakota
woman was given. Missionaries called
her Nancy, which means "grace," and
she is known to history as Nancy
Eastman. When she was seventeen,
Winona married a Dakota man
named Many Lightnings, but the
missionaries knew him as Jacob Eastman. They lived in
Cloud Man's village, near Gideon Pond's home, then
moved later to a reservation on the Minnesota River.

Winona

Winona/Great Spirit Woman had one daughter
and four sons. She died in the spring of 1858, after her
last child was born. Her youngest child, Charles
Alexander Eastman, graduated as a medical doctor from
Dartmouth College and Boston University. He also
served his people through the Bureau of Indian Affairs
and became a famous writer of books on North
American Indians.

Some of Cloud Man's descendants still live in
the Shakopee area, where
Samuel Pond established his
mission, and are members of
the Mdewakanton communi-
ty there. Others live in the
Twin Cities and several serve
on the Native American
Advisory Board for the Gibbs
Farm Museum.

Cloud Man

Whether Jane ever saw the Pond brothers or Winona again is uncertain, but she did maintain her friendship with the Dakota people for many years. As the Dakota traveled north for their annual rice gathering, they would pause at Jane's farm home where she would host as many as a hundred people for three weeks at a time. Her kitchen floor often would be covered with sleeping men, and Jane's daughter remembered Jane jumping over their feet and teasing them in Dakota. She traded with them, her vegetables and melons for their cranberries and rice, and she gave fresh bread to anyone who was hungry.

Jane understood that the growth of white settlement and often restrictive government policies caused great suffering for her friends. She was deeply saddened when they last visited her in May of 1862, only months before the outbreak of the fighting between white settlers and several Dakota bands that is known as the Dakota Conflict. Dwight Stevens also experienced the tragedy of warfare. He did realize his dream of becoming a soldier. He served in the Union army during the Civil War. Less than a year after the end of the Dakota Conflict, he lost his life in the Battle of Gettysburg in 1863.

Heman Gibbs died in 1891. Jane remained at their farm home until she died there on May 30, 1910, surrounded by her family.

Pond Brothers' Cabin

Lake of
the Isles

Lake
Calhoun

Ponds' Cabin

Cloud Man's
Village

Mission House
and School

Lake
Harriet

If you live in Minneapolis or St. Paul, or if you visit there, you can follow this map to see the sights Jane saw and walk where Jane walked as a child along the shores of Lake Calhoun and Lake Harriet. The location of the schoolhouse is marked by a plaque set into a low bank at the northwest corner of Lake Harriet, near the bandstand. Labeled "First Schoolhouse in Minneapolis," the plaque credits Reverend J. D. Stevens and Gideon Pond with building it, but does not mention the nearby Mission House. Cloud Man's village also was nearby, on land that is now part of Lakewood Cemetery. The Ponds' cabin on Lake Calhoun was close to the site today of St. Mary's Orthodox Church. Look for the church with the golden dome. A plaque marking the cabin site is attached to a boulder on the lakeshore below the church.

The Gibbs Farm Museum, Jane's home as a wife and mother, is a National Historic Site. It stands at the corner of Cleveland and Larpenteur avenues in the northern St. Paul suburb of Falcon Heights in Ramsey County. There you will see the location of the sod and log dugout shanty, Jane's first home, and the farmhouse itself, with some of the furnishings that belonged to Jane. In the fields behind the farmhouse, you will see a Dakota tioti surrounded by a Dakota garden, much like the garden Jane helped tend in Cloud Man's village so many years ago.

Acknowledgments

This book would not have been possible without the help of Jane herself. Her own stories of her remarkable childhood were recorded by her daughter, Lillie Belle Gibbs LeVesconte, in *Little Bird That Was Caught, A Story of the Early Years of Jane DeBow Gibbs*, published first in 1954 and again in 1968 by the Ramsey County Historical Society. Jane comes alive today through living-history portrayals by Karen Bluhm, Jane's great, great granddaughter, who often appears as Jane at the Gibbs Farm Museum.

Jane also comes to life again in these pages through author Anne Neuberger's careful research and skillful writing that have woven together the many threads of Jane's early years. With her delightful sketches, artist Tessie Bundick has recreated Jane's long-ago world; and designer Mark Odegard has guided the project from manuscript to printed page.

The Ramsey County Historical Society wishes to express its deep appreciation to the many other people and organizations who also helped make this book possible: The Patrick and Aimee Butler Family Foundation and the Helen Lang Charitable Trust, whose support was critical in launching the book; Vicenta D. Scarlett in memory of her mother, Vicenta C. Donnelly; Arthur Baumeister, Jr.; Laurie Murphy; and the Board of Ramsey County Commissioners—Susan Haigh, chair, Tony Bennett, Dino Guerin, Rafael Ortega, Victoria Reinhardt, Janice Rettman, and Jan Wiessner—whose steadfast support of the Ramsey County Historical

Society through the years has helped maintain Jane's old home as the Gibbs Farm Museum.

We also are greatly indebted to a special group of people whose wise guidance has helped the Society tell the story of Jane Gibbs and her Dakota friends. They are the members of the Native American Advisory Board for the Gibbs Farm Museum and they include descendants of some of the real people in our story:

Gary Cavender, *Shungui* (Red Fox), Dakota, Prior Lake, Minnesota, direct descendant of Cloud Man, who holds Cloud Man's pipe;

Gabrielle Strong, *Tahniya Wakan Win* (Sacred Breath Woman), Dakota, St. Paul, direct descendant of Cloud Man;

David Larsen, *Shpu Shpu Wicasta* (Scabby), Dakota, Prior Lake, descendant of Wabasha;

Linda Owen, Dakota, Welch, Minnesota, descendant of Wabasha;

Roger Buffalohead, Ponca, Minneapolis;

Paul Durand, Prior Lake, author of *Where the Rivers Meet and Waters Flow*;

Patty Thompson, *Zitkadan To Win* (Bluebird Lady), Dakota, North St. Paul, direct descendant of Cloud Man;

Yvonne Leith, *Mazaokiyewin* (Woman Who Speaks to Iron), Dakota, St. Paul, direct descendant of Cloud Man;

232

Lisa Owen, *Dowan Wakan Win* (Sings Holy Woman), Dakota, Hastings, Minnesota, descendant of Seth Eastman.

Dale Weston, *Mahpiya Wicasta* (Cloud Man), St. Paul, descendant of Cloud Man;

Michael Scullin, professor of anthropology, Mankato State University;

Consultant: Vernell Wabasha, Dakota, Morton, Minnesota.

RCHS executive director, and Virginia Brainard Kunz, editor of the Society's quarterly magazine, *Ramsey County History*.

For the staff of the Ramsey County Historical Society, this has been an absorbing project: Priscilla Farnham has guided the project since its inception two years ago; Virginia Kunz edited the manuscript through countless drafts; Ted Lau, manager of the Gibbs Farm Museum, Tom LaBlanc, Gibbs Farm Museum interpreter, and Mollie Spillman, RCHS archivist, both provided important research; Eleanor Arnason, accountant, kept her eye on the all-important finances.

We also thank those who cheerfully shared their own knowledge of Jane's life and times. Dr. Keith Widder's doctoral thesis on Evangelical Protestants at Mackinac Island shed much light on Reverend Stevens' sojourn there. Deanne Zibell Weber's article, "A Pioneer Child on Minnesota's Frontier..." traced Jane's childhood and later life for the spring, 1996, issue of *Ramsey County History*.

Last but never least, we wish to thank those who have read the manuscript and offered important comments and criticisms: Jay Red Hawk; Gary Cavender; and Roger Buffalohead; Terry Nelson, librarian at St. Mary of the Lake School in White Bear Lake; and Mary Lou Evanoff and Nancy Guertin, teacher and librarian at Holy Family Middle School in St. Paul.

Above all, we salute our youngest readers and helpful critics, these fourth-through-seventh scholars from a number of Twin Cities schools: Dan Banken, Emma Clabo, Robert H. Farnham, Annelise Hoyland, Brendan Kelley, Jenny Kohler, Etta Langer, Caitlin Laszewski, Lucia and Elizabeth Marincel, Clare, Sarah and Madeline Neenan, Paul and Jack Roos, Bill Sand, Teresa Scherping, Scott Toskey, Autumn Valentine, and Katelyn Weichelt. It was for them and their fellow readers that this book really was written.

Read more about Jane's Era

BOOKS:
Ault, Phil. *Whistles Round the Bend, Travel on America's Waterways.* New York: Dodd, Mead and Company, 1982.

Blegen, Theodore C. *Minnesota, A History of the State.* Minneapolis: University of Minnesota Press, 1963, 1975.

Blegen, Theodore C., and Philip D. Jordan. *With Various Voices, Recordings of North Star Life.* St. Paul: The Itasca Press, 1949.

Boehme, Sarah E., Christian F. Feest, and Patricia Condon Johnston. *Seth Eastman, A Portfolio of North American Indians.* Afton, Minnesota: Afton Historical Society Press, 1995.

Eastman, Mary, illustrated by Seth Eastman. *Dahcotah, Life and Legends of the Sioux.* Minneapolis: Ross, Haines, Inc., 1849, 1962.

Greene, Jacqueline D. *The Chippewa.* New York: Franklin Watts, 1993.

Hall, Stephen P. *Fort Snelling, Colossus of the Wilderness.* St.Paul: Minnesota Historical Society Press, 1987.

Hansen, Marcus L. *Old Fort Snelling.* Minneapolis: Ross and Haines, Inc., 1958.

Hanson, Jeffrey R, ed. *Buffalo Bird Woman's Garden: Agriculture of the Hidatsa Indians,* as told to Gilbert L. Wilson. St. Paul: Minnesota Historical Society Press, 1987.

Hassrick, Royal B., in collaboration with Dorothy Maxwell and Cile M. Bach. *The Sioux, Life and Customs of a Warrior Society.* Norman, Oklahoma, and London: University of Oklahoma Press, 1964.

Kinzie, Juliette M., *Wau-Bun-The "Early Day" in the Northwest.* The Collegiate Press: Menasha, Wisconsin, 1968.

Lettermann, Edward J. *From Whole Log to No Log, A History of the Indians Where the Mississippi and the Minnesota Rivers Meet.* Minneapolis: Dillon Press, 1969.

Lucus, Eileen. *The Ojibwas, People of the Northern Forests.* Brookfield, Connecticut: Millbrook Press, 1994.

Pond, Samuel W. *The Dakota or Sioux in Minnesota As They Were in 1834.* St. Paul: Minnesota Historical Society Press: 1908, 1986.

Riggs, Maida Leonard, ed. *A Small Bit of Bread and Butter: Letters from the Dakota Territory, 1832–1869.* South Deerfield, MA: Ash Grove Press, 1966.

Robison, Mabel Otis. *Minnesota Pioneers, Word Pictures of Famous Characters and Interesting Events in the Story of Minnesota.* Minneapolis: T.S. Denison and Company.

Whitcomb, Charlotte, "A Pioneer Woman" 1958. Obituary of Jane Debow Gibbs originally published in the *Minneapolis Journal,* June 26, 1897. Edited and annotated by Edward J. Lettermann, 1965.

Widder, Keith Robert. *Together as Family: Metis Children's Response to Evangelical Protestants at the Mackinaw Mission, 1823-1837.* Ann Arbor: a Dissertation submitted to Michigan State University, 1989.

PERIODICAL:
Weber, Deanne Zibell. "A Pioneer Child on Minnesota's Frontier, Jane Gibbs, the 'Little Bird That Was Caught,' and Her Dakota Friends." *Ramsey County History,* Vol. 31, No. 1. St. Paul: Ramsey County Historical Society, Spring 1996.

AUDIO TAPE:
Bonnie Goodbird Wells, narrator. *Buffalo Bird Woman, My Life on the Northern Plains 1840-1890.* Bismarck, South Dakota: Meyer Creative Productions, 1994.

PAMPHLETS:
LeVesconte, Lillie Belle Gibbs. *Little Bird That Was Caught, A Story of the Early Years of Jane DeBow Gibbs,* by her daughter Lillie Belle Gibbs LeVesconte. St. Paul: Ramsey Country Historical Society, 1968.

Dakota Garden, St. Paul: Ramsey County Historical Society, 1997. Educational Brochure.

Native American Tipi, St. Paul, Ramsey County Historical Society. Educational Brochure.

Anne Neuberger grew up in Nekoosa, Wisconsin, where as a child she spent hours reading, writing, and drawing. She is a graduate of St. Mary's University in Winona, and lives in St. Paul with her husband, four children, "lots of books and two pet rabbits." She is the author of two earlier books for young readers: *Advent Stories and Activities, Meeting Jesus Through the Jesse Tree,* and *The Girl-Son,* which has been nominated for the 1998-1999 Maud Hart Lovelace Book Award.

Tessie Bundick, illustrator and artist, also designs make-up and costumes for theater, film, and television productions in the Twin Cities. This book is the fourth published children's book she has illustrated.